Editor
Dona Rice

Editorial Project Manager
Karen J. Goldfluss, M.S. Ed.

Editor-in-Chief
Sharon Coan, M.S. Ed.

Illustrator
Barb Lorseyedi

Cover Artist
Denise Bauer

Art Coordinator
Cheri Macoubrie Wilson

Creative Director
Elayne Roberts

Associate Designer
Denise Bauer

Imaging
Ralph Olmedo, Jr.

Product Manager
Phil Garcia

Publisher
Mary D. Smith, M.S. Ed.

Writing Works

Lessons and Activities for the Writing Process

Grades K–3

Author

Karen King

Teacher Created Resources, Inc.
6421 Industry Way
Westminster, CA 92683
www.teachercreated.com
ISBN: 978-1-57690-009-3
©1998 Teacher Created Resources, Inc.
Reprinted, 2010
Made in U.S.A.

Table of Contents

Building Background for a Writing Workshop

Introduction

When writing is a part of every day, children develop an understanding that reading, writing, and speaking are connected parts of language.

Building background knowledge for a writing workshop begins the first day of school. Every time a story is read to the children or writing takes place, background knowledge for a writing workshop begins to develop for the children. Everything done and said while reading a story to the children relates to what they will do when they write their own stories. Everything done and said when writing to or with the children relates to what they will do when they write independently.

When the teacher writes in front of the students, he or she. . .

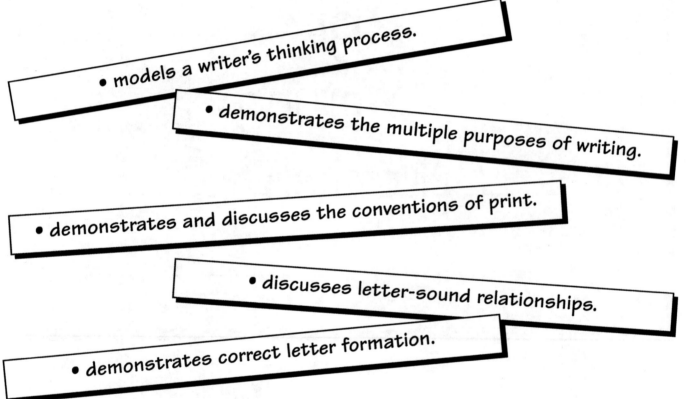

- models a writer's thinking process.
- demonstrates the multiple purposes of writing.
- demonstrates and discusses the conventions of print.
- discusses letter-sound relationships.
- demonstrates correct letter formation.

Writing lessons developed to build background are of two types—those that teach correct mechanics and those designed to teach the craft of writing. Lessons that focus on correct mechanics deal with spelling, letter formation, and punctuation. Lessons that focus on developing the student's craft of writing deal with improving and expanding the student's writing.

The activities in this section should be incorporated into the curriculum and teaching day whenever and however appropriate. They do not need to be taught as individual lessons nor do they need to be taught as written. Glean what you can that works for you and your students.

Reading a Story

Every time you read a story to the students, you have an opportunity to develop background knowledge that they will use when writing their own stories. Below are some ideas for building background when reading a story. Do not incorporate all of the ideas each time a story is shared; be selective and specific. Prereading the story will help determine which ideas are best to use. The ideas will need to be repeated often to become part of the children's background knowledge for your writing workshop.

Ideas for Building Background

- **Point out the title and the author's name on the book cover.**

- **Point out the location of the capital and lowercase letters in the title.**

- **Ask children to make predictions about the story.**

- **Instruct the children to justify their predictions with supporting information.**

- **Discuss the elements of the story:**

    —setting (where and when)

    —characters (who)

    —problem (the central difficulty that must be resolved)

    —solution (how the problem is solved)

- **Discuss the parts of a story:**

    —beginning (setting and character introduction)

    —middle (character development and problem)

    —end (solution of the problem and denouement)

- **Point out things that make the story interesting:**

    —illustrations

    —descriptive and figurative language

- **Name the various parts of the book:**

    —cover

    —title page

    —dedication page

    —author information page

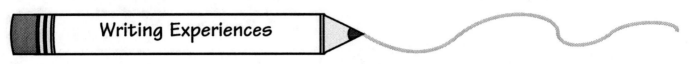

Writing Experiences

The children's preschool experiences with writing will vary. Each student will have reached a different point on the continuum of writing development. The goal is to encourage the children's development along the continuum in a safe and supportive environment, realizing that they will swing back and forth among the stages as they move.

Stages on the Continuum of Writing Development

1. **Drawing Pictures:** Children begin by drawing pictures to express their thoughts.

2. **Scribbling:** As they observe adults writing, they begin to scribble as an imitation of what they observe. The modeling they have observed has taught them that what is written can be read. They take their scribbling to an adult to read it, believing that the knowledge of what has been written lies with the reader. They will not be able to tell the reader what it says.

3. **Making Letter-Like Forms:** As they more closely observe adults writing, children begin to intermix some letter-like forms with their scribbling. They continue to believe the knowledge of what has been written lies within the reader.

4. **Random Lettering:** Children begin making random letters or strings of letters as a form of writing. The knowledge of what they have written begins to become the children's responsibility. They are able to identify for an adult the word(s) represented by the letter(s). Most children have reached this stage of writing development when they enter kindergarten.

5. **Invented Spelling:** As the children are praised and encouraged through the previous stage, they begin to make sound-symbol relationships and move into "invented spelling." (Invented spelling will hereafter be referred to as developmental spelling because it is a process of developing. The approximations make sense and can be analyzed.) Although the children accept more responsibility for the knowledge of what has been written, the reader will be looked to for help. Once the children move closer to the next stage, they are often unable to read what they have written at the beginning of this stage. It is during this stage that children will write labels (single words), phrases, and sentences. They will also begin making lists which may use a similar word or many of the same words in each phrase or sentence. Children need a great deal of positive encouragement to move on to writing sentences that contain different but connected ideas about a topic.

6. **Conventional Spelling:** Children (and adults) move between the previous stage and this one, depending on the difficulty of the words being used in the writing. It is only at the conventional spelling stage that the writer becomes completely responsible for the knowledge of what has been written.

Writing Experiences

Monthly Journals and Sustained Silent Writing

Sustained Silent Writing (SSW) is similar to Sustained Silent Reading (SSR). It is a specific time each day set aside for the children to do "free" writing, writing that is unguided and ungraded. The children, however, are expected to do their best work.

Sharing writing encourages children to develop their writing skills. It is useful to use a variety of methods to allow children to share their work.

Students can share their writing in the following ways:

- with the partner next to him or her
- with the whole group
- with the partner across from him or her
- with a partner of choice
- with a partner drawn at random
- with a small group
- in a "donut" (One group of children forms a circle with their backs to the middle, and the other children form a circle around them.)

SSW can be done in a journal used expressly for that purpose. Journals are made by stapling several pieces of paper between construction paper covers. The children can be given a new journal each month. Different colored construction paper each month makes the journals easy to organize for "Reflections on Writing" at the end of the year. Monthly journals can be sent home to be shared at the end of each month with a letter to the parent requesting that they be returned the next day. If desired, you can also ask the parents to write a response to the journals before returning them. Their responses can be addressed to their children.

Writing Experiences

Monthly Journals and Sustained Silent Writing *(cont.)*

The following information is geared toward the use of journals in specific grade levels.

Kindergarten

Begin by using blank paper on which the children draw a picture. Sharing their pictures with classmates gives them an audience for whom to draw and helps them to develop their verbal skills. The next step for them is to use a word or words to label their pictures. Afterwards, they can begin to use paper with one or more writing lines, drawing a picture and writing about it on the line(s). Support the children's use of "kindergarten spelling" (writing the letters whose sounds they hear when they say the word). This is a normal and vital step toward the development of conventional spelling.

First Grade

In first grade, children build upon their kindergarten experience. If they did not experience journal writing in kindergarten, begin with blank paper for pictures and labels. Decrease the size of the picture portion of the page each month, completely eliminating the picture portion by midyear. Since the emphasis of SSW after the first month of school should clearly be writing, encourage children to write before they draw a picture. Support the children's use of "first grade spelling" (writing any letter sounds they hear when they say the word). Again, this is a normal and necessary step to conventional spelling.

Second Grade

The children will again build on their prior experiences, using a format similar to that used at the end of first grade. If the children have not had previous journal writing experiences, begin during the first month with paper allowing a small picture area. Move to a fully lined page during the following months. Support the children's use of "second grade spelling" (writing conventionally any words they have previously learned and writing down letter sounds they hear when they say the word for any others). This step brings them very close to complete conventional spelling.

Third Grade

By the third grade, the students should have had a fair amount of writing experience. Build on this prior experience, using a format similar to what was used at the end of second grade. Provide fully lined paper for their writing, forgoing drawing in lieu of complete written content. Require a reasonable amount of conventional spelling, allowing for invented spellings wherever necessary so as not to interrupt the flow of ideas onto paper. Remember, spelling can always be corrected, and a primary purpose of sustained writing is to encourage fluidity of thought and expression. Stopping to look up words in the dictionary will sometimes block that flow.

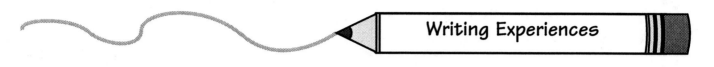

Daily Newsletter

The daily newsletter is an opportunity to develop and improve the children's literacy skills and to build their self-esteem. Reading, writing, and speaking skills are developed through this activity. Many reading, writing, and spelling skills can be directly taught through the daily newsletter.

The daily newsletter demonstrates to the children that what they say can be written down. It places importance on the things the children share verbally. It is a wonderful opportunity to develop the children's speaking skills and their internal development of the rules that govern our language. It is also useful in building their vocabulary.

Details about creating a daily newsletter for the various grade levels are included below and on the next two pages. Additionally, the final section of every newsletter can be devoted to "Parent News" which offers the teacher an opportunity to communicate with parents on a daily basis. The space is limited, allowing only one or two sentences, and the communication is informal, but it does go a long way in keeping in contact with parents. It can be used to keep parents abreast of the learning activities taking place in the classroom, to elicit volunteer help, and to remind parents of upcoming events pertaining to the classroom.

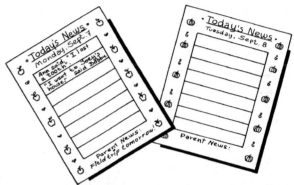

Ann said, "I lost a tooth."

"I went to Joey's house," said Bobby.

Kindergarten

Incorporate the writing of the daily newsletter with "show and tell" sharing time. After each of the children has shared, the teacher states one sentence that tells the most important points shared. The teacher then writes that sentence on the chalkboard. After several months of modeling this technique, the teacher can ask for a volunteer to give the sentence. The children then do a choral reading of all the sentences with the teacher.

Whatever time of day you choose, make the daily newsletter a regular practice. If possible, have an aide or parent volunteer copy the sentences on a sheet of paper together with your parent news and send the newsletter home. To simplify, send it home weekly as the "Weekly News," including a news statement from each child.

Use this as an opportunity to emphasize beginning consonant sounds, high frequency words, "talk marks" (quotation marks), left to right/up to down reading, capital letters and end punctuation, and any words from your reading program.

The sentences can be used in a variety of other ways. For example, they can be

- written on sentence strips and used for repeated readings.
- made into a class book by writing each child's sentence on a page, which the child illustrates.
- compiled and sent home weekly.

Writing Experiences

Daily Newsletter *(cont.)*

First Grade

Use the daily newsletter as an alternative to show-and-tell sharing. First grade children can develop their public speaking skills as well as their reading, writing, and spelling skills through the daily newsletter by reporting "news" once a week. Ask them to share news that is important to the world, their town, their school, or themselves, and limit each child's news to one sentence. (For most first grade children this is very difficult. As with all skills, practice improves their ability.)

Appropriate writing forms are naturally modeled by the teacher when writing each child's news sentence on the chalkboard. Sentences should be written in the children's exact words. The children are then encouraged to expound on their news once the sentence is written.

When all news has been given, the newsletter is read aloud in unison. During the day, the newsletter is photocopied for each child. Before taking the newsletter home to share with parents, the children practice reading it several times.

Use this as an opportunity to emphasize vowel sounds, high frequency words, words from the reading program, nouns, verbs, capitalization and punctuation, conventional spelling of commonly used words, and other skills you might be studying.

The daily newsletter is an excellent alternative to the daily oral language activity traditionally done in first grade classrooms. To expand upon it and to provide even greater enrichment, begin to make mistakes in the writing of the news on the chalkboard (as the year progresses and the students become better readers). For example, omit a capital letter, periods, quotation marks, commas, and so forth. Begin by telling the children how many mistakes there are in each sentence, then in the entire newsletter, and then simply that there are mistakes. This is a powerful activity, and you will find the carry-over into their own writing significant. (**Note:** When rewriting the newsletter on the form for photocopying, do not make mistakes.)

Second and Third Grades

The daily newsletter at this level is used as an opportunity to develop the children's independent writing skills. Children act as reporters and assume responsibility for the writing of the newsletter. The reporters for the day write the news on a form provided by the teacher.

The teacher photocopies one for each of the children. The children practice reading the newsletter before it is taken home to be shared with parents.

Teaching opportunities at this level include teaching high frequency words, words from the reading program, nouns, verbs, capitalization and punctuation, conventional spelling of commonly used words, dictionary skills, and more.

(Note: If the children do not have prior newsletter experience, the second or third grade teacher should spend several months modeling the writing of the newsletter before turning over the responsibility to the children.)

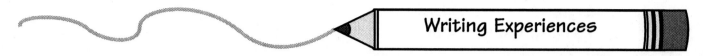

Here is a daily news master for you to use.

Today's News

Date:

_____   _____

_____   _____

_____   _____

_____   _____

_____   _____

_____   _____

_____   _____

_____   _____

_____   _____

_____   _____

_____   _____

_____   _____

Parent News: _____

_____

Writing Experiences

Class Books

To make a class book, each student contributes one page. A cover is usually provided by the teacher. Class books can be distributed to the children at the end of the year, or they can be taken apart, each child receiving his or her page from each class book. They can be made in a number of ways: stapled, stapled and taped, spiral bound, held together with rings, tied with string, and more. The manner should best suit the method in which books or pages will be distributed at the end of the year. If each child will take home his or her pages from each book, arrange the pages of each book alphabetically by the children's last names. This will make it easier to return their pages at the end of the year. While the books remain intact, they can become a part of the classroom library.

Class books are an excellent extension activity to a lesson, to a piece of literature, or to any other common experience.

Kindergarten

Class books in kindergarten can be made in a variety of ways. The following are suggestions:

- A picture on a specific topic can be drawn by the child and labeled by the child, teacher, or helper. Topics might include a specific initial consonant sound, sports, families, a color, and so forth.

- A frame sentence can be provided, and each child completes the sentence by adding one or more words and an illustration to the page.

- A script or story can be divided into parts, and each child can illustrate his or her story section or line of script.

Class Books *(cont.)*

First Grade

Class books in first grade can be made in a variety of ways. The following are suggestions:

- At the beginning of the year, provide a frame sentence in which each child completes the sentence by adding several words. Instruct each child to add an appropriate illustration to his or her page to complete it.

- Sentence starters work well for class books and offer first grade children more opportunity to individualize their pages. All class books that require the children to write help to develop their skills and confidence as authors. The children complete the pages by adding illustrations.

- Talking bubbles as part of the illustration can be used for writing on each child's page. (The easiest way to do this is to teach the children to do the writing first and then to draw the bubble around the words.)

- Class language experience stories can become a class book by dividing the story into the needed number of parts. The words for each part can be written or typed on separate pages. The children can add illustrations to the words on each page.

This type of structured writing needs to become more sophisticated as the children's abilities develop.

Second Grade

Class books at this level are usually topic-based, such as a book of thoughts about fall, poems, or sports. The emphasis of these class books is creative expression. Each child's page consists of one or more paragraphs, the emphasis being on the children's creativity, appropriate use of grammar and mechanics, correct spelling, and handwriting. An illustration may be added or a teacher-provided border may be colored. As the children's writing abilities develop, this type of structured writing should become more sophisticated. These books are bound, and they should become a part of the class library.

Third Grade

Class books at this level can be topic-based, a collection of student poems or stories, or a story written by the whole class (or one page per student). Students should be accountable for correct spelling, grammar, and form, as well as neatness in their presentation. Student illustrations can be included, but they are not mandatory. Bind the final books and include them in the class library. If possible, allow the class to read the books to other classes in your school, visiting parents, or a nearby preschool.

Writing Experiences

Sequence Picture Story

This is a two-step activity. It can be done in one session, although this is not recommended. Allowing two separate sessions helps to maintain the children's interest.

During session one, the children are given a sheet containing three or four pictures that are out of sequential order. The children color and cut out the pictures. Then they are glued onto another sheet of paper in the proper sequential order. During session two, the children are given their sequenced pictures and a sheet of writing paper. Using the pictures to generate ideas, the children write about the pictures.

Kindergarten

Although session one of this activity can be done early in the year, the children will probably not be ready for session two until near the end of the year. Even at the end of the year, some children will need assistance with the writing.

When doing this activity with kindergartners, the pictures should be simple, allowing the children to label each picture with only a few words. When complete, the sequenced pictures and writing should be shared and celebrated as the children's first stories.

First Grade

The writing paper given to first grade children should be premarked with every other line numbered (1–4). On this paper, the children will create a story about the provided pictures by writing one sentence about each picture on the corresponding lines. These should be shared and celebrated as the children's original stories.

Second Grade

At this grade level the children need not be required to color the pictures to be sequenced. Early in the year, the children can complete this activity in the same way they might have done it in first grade. As the year progresses, the children should be required to write a paragraph about each picture. This is an excellent opportunity to teach paragraph writing. The completed stories should be shared and celebrated as the children's original stories.

Third Grade

Begin at a level comfortable for the students, somewhere just prior to where they left off in second grade. From there, progress to the writing of at least one paragraph per picture as well as an appropriate introduction and conclusion. Third grade writing should show clear sequence, good paragraph transitions, and correct grammar and form. Also, cross over the sequential-story concept to other areas of the curriculum, providing students the opportunity to develop essays on such topics as the development of a flower from seed to blossom or the process of a bill becoming a law.

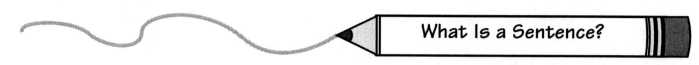

What Is a Sentence?

Parts of a Sentence

Activity:

The class will identify the parts of a sentence.

Materials:

- chalkboard or overhead projector

Preparation:

Write a sentence that the children can read on the chalkboard or overhead projector.

Directions:

Instruct the students that a sentence is a group of words that tell who or what and what happened. Then, think aloud, "Let me think about this sentence. If this is really a sentence, it will make sense, tell something, and sound good. I should be able to tell about whom or what it is telling me. I should also be able to tell what is happening in the sentence. I think I will draw a circle around the words that tell about whom or what. Now, what is happening in the sentence? I can draw a circle around the words that tell me what is happening."

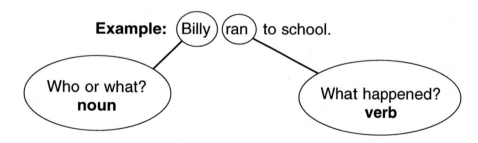

Instruct the children to provide sample sentences. Repeat the "think aloud" process for each sentence.

When the students are ready, instruct them to "think aloud."

Note: It will be very obvious when a group of words is not a sentence. One or both of the elements (noun or verb) will be missing.

Examples:

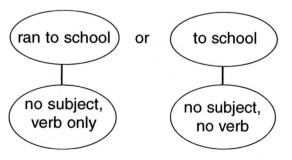

What Is a Sentence?

Declarative Sentences

Activity:

Each student will state a declarative sentence in a game called Tell Me Something.

Materials:

- none

Preparation:

No preparation is needed.

Directions:

Define and model declarative sentences for the students. A declarative sentence is a statement that tells something and ends with a period. Sample declarative sentences include the following:

The dog ran through the park.

I am wearing a blue dress.

The weather is windy and cold today.

If desired, call the sentences "telling sentences" if you feel your students will not be able to grasp the term "declarative."

Tell Me Something

After explaining declarative sentences, play Tell Me Something with the children. To play, instruct the students to sit in a circle. Ask for a volunteer to go first. This child "tells something." (The statement can be anything as long as it is declarative.) The child can tell only one sentence, and there are no responses given. Next, continue to ask for volunteers or proceed around the circle. Do not forget to include yourself. (The children enjoy learning things about you, too.)

To expand the activity and to reinforce the term "declarative" in the students' minds, ask them to preface their statements with the phrase, "I declare." Since the accessibility of vocabulary is basically a matter of exposure, the students' use of the term will make likely its addition to their own lexicons.

The benefits of playing Tell Me Something are manifold. It provides an excellent means by which to build the children's confidence and self-esteem, to develop their oral language skills, and to increase their ease when speaking publicly.

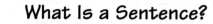

What Is a Sentence?

Interrogative Sentences

Activity:

Each student will state an interrogative sentence in a game called Ask Something.

Materials:

- none

Preparation:

No preparation is needed.

Directions:

An interrogative sentence is a sentence that asks something and requires an answer. It ends with a question mark. Explain this to the students and model an interrogative sentence for them.

Then, play the game Ask Something with the children. To play, instruct the students to sit in a circle. Ask for a volunteer to go first. This child "asks something" of anyone in the group. (The sentence can be anything as long as it is interrogative.) The child can ask only one question. The group gives a "thumbs up" if the sentence is interrogative. If not, the child can try again. After the silent signal, the question may be answered by the one of whom it is asked.

Ask Something

Next, continue to ask for volunteers or proceed around the circle. Do not forget to include yourself.

To extend this activity, ask an interrogative of each student in your class and have each respond with a declarative.

As with Tell Me Something, this activity is an excellent way to build the children's confidence and self-esteem, develop their oral language skills, and increase their ease when speaking publicly. Also, the children develop a better understanding of the difference between "telling" and "asking" sentences when they play this game.

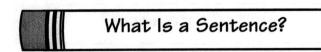

What Is a Sentence?

Have a Question?

Activity:

In either small groups or as a whole class, the students will play Have a Question?, a game that reinforces the distinction between declarative (telling) and interrogative (asking) sentences.

Materials:

- question word cards (pages 19 and 20)
- paper bag

Preparation:

1. Copy, laminate, and cut out the word cards.
2. Decorate the paper bag.
3. Place the word cards in the bag.

Directions:

Instruct one child at a time to draw a question word card from the bag. The child reads his or her word aloud and then orally begins a sentence with the word. Point out that the sentences are interrogative or asking sentences.

Proceed around the room or group so that everyone has an opportunity to play. Keep the question bag handy and practice often. If a particular child has difficulty distinguishing or stating questions, have him or her work with a partner or classroom aide to get additional practice.

To increase the challenge of the activity, make additional cards with words that are not likely to begin a question. When the child makes a statement, ask the rest of the class to identify the type of statement made.

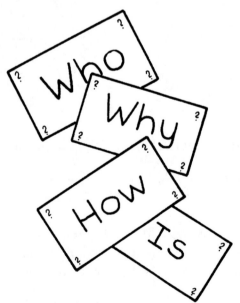

What Is a Sentence?

Word Cards for Have a Question?

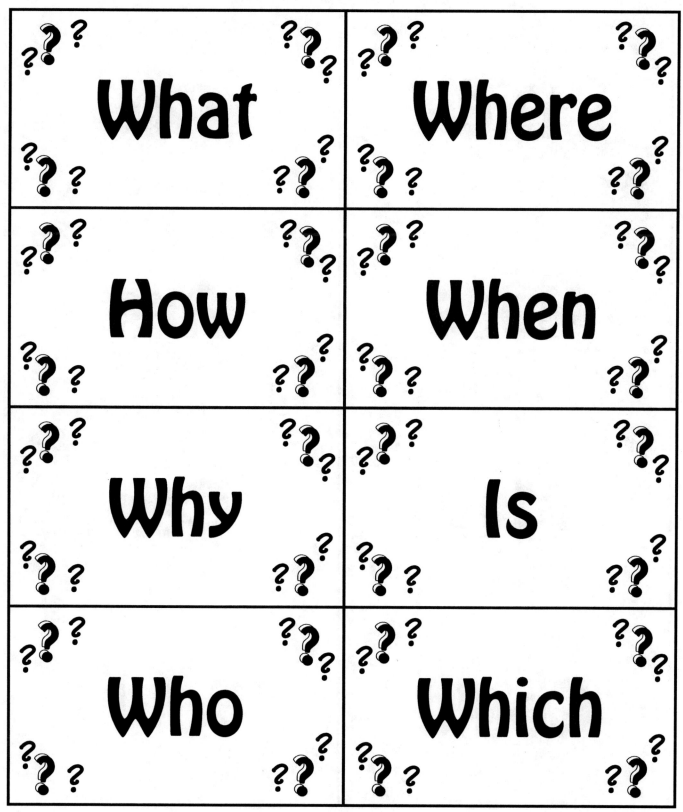

What	Where
How	When
Why	Is
Who	Which

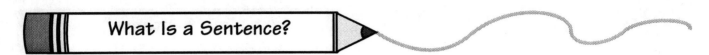

What Is a Sentence?

Word Cards for Have a Question? *(cont.)*

What Is a Sentence?

Pieces, Pieces, Pieces

Activity:

This activity allows the students to use their own creativity and imaginations to write sentences.

Materials:

- pieces from a jigsaw puzzle (at least 1 piece per child)
- writing paper
- pencils

Preparation:

No preparation is needed.

Directions:

Give each child a piece from the same puzzle. Have each child look at the puzzle piece and try to visualize the entire puzzle picture. After they have spent a few moments thinking and imagining, instruct them each to write a sentence or paragraph describing the entire puzzle. When complete, have the students share their writing.

Afterwards, allow the children to finish the puzzle to discover what the complete picture looks like. Be sure to include any pieces not previously distributed. You may wish to follow through with a discussion about what they imagined and how it compares to the actual puzzle.

To vary this activity, have the students tell about their own pieces and share their written sentences or paragraphs. When they have finished, put everyone's writing together. In this way, you will combine the pieces of writing just as one would combine the pieces of the puzzle. This is an excellent opportunity for teaching how sentences work together to communicate.

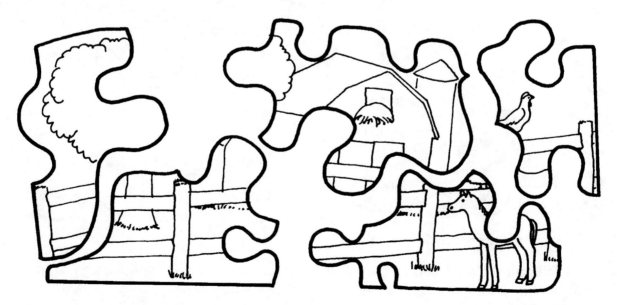

What Is a Sentence?

Look Who's Talking!

Activity:

The students will write dialogues.

Materials:

- magazine pictures featuring 2 or more people or animals (at least 1 per child)
- large pieces of construction paper (1 per child)

- writing paper
- pencils
- glue

Preparation:

1. Trim the pictures for mounting.

2. Prepare a completed sample.

Directions:

Let each child select a picture and a piece of construction paper. The construction paper should be larger than the picture, allowing for a wide border. The children may need to glue their writings in the borders.

Using writing paper, each child should write a statement or question for each person or animal in the picture. After writing each statement, the child should draw a conversation bubble around it and cut it out. When all bubbles have been cut, instruct the children to glue their pictures to the construction paper and then to glue the bubbles near the appropriate speakers, using the construction frame as needed.

You may wish to show the children ahead of time how they can alter the conversation bubbles to show spoken words or thoughts.

spoken words   **thoughts**

When complete, allow the students to share their work, creating voices for the characters, if they wish. Display the writing for future reading under the title "Look Who's Talking!"

What Is a Sentence?

Picture File Stories

Activity:

The students will write original sentences or paragraphs about a common picture. All work will be collected into a class book.

Materials:

- large color picture from a calendar, magazine, newspaper, etc.
- chart paper and marking pen
- writing paper
- pencils

Preparation:

Select and display the picture.

Directions:

Display the picture so the children can see it clearly. Then ask the children to brainstorm for things they see and think about the picture. Record their ideas on chart paper, sorting the ideas into topic groups while recording them.

When complete, have each child write a sentence or paragraph about the picture, using their brainstormed responses. Share the finished writing in small groups or as a class. Discuss the similarities and differences of the writing and how each person's is at least a little bit different from everyone else's. This is a good opening to some basic discussion of point of view.

Display the children's writings by stacking them and stapling them together to the bottom of the picture, creating a book. Hang the picture book in a location where the children can easily read the stories.

Brown Bear's Day at the Beach

Yesterday, Brown Bear went to the beach. He had so much fun.

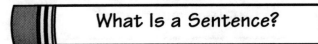
What Is a Sentence?

Very "Apple-tizing"

Activity:

This activity for small groups or at a center challenges the students to differentiate between complete and incomplete sentences.

Materials:

- file folder (1 per group or several if at a center)
- as many apple shapes as desired
- tree pattern (1 per file folder)
- marking pen
- colored pencils, crayons, or markers
- scissors
- laminating machine
- basket (1 per group or only 1 if at a center)

Preparation:

1. Color and cut out the trees.

2. Attach one completed tree to the inside of each file folder. Label the tree "Complete Sentences" and the ground area around the tree "Incomplete Sentences." Laminate the folder for durability.

3. Copy the apples onto colored paper (red, green, or yellow). Write a complete or an incomplete sentence that the children are able to read on each apple. Laminate them for durability and cut them out.

4. Place the apples in a basket.

Directions:

Instruct the students to read the sentences on the apples. They can then sort the apples by stacking them on the tree if the words form a complete sentence or on the ground around the tree if the sentence is incomplete.

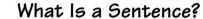

What Is a Sentence?

Punctuation, Please!

Activity:

The students will add punctuation to previously written text while in a small group or center.

Materials:

- file folder (1 per child)
- glue stick (1 per child)
- optional: pictures to accompany stories
- teacher-created, reproducible stories
- wipe-off marker (1 per child)

Preparation:

1. Write several sets of two- or three-sentence stories, omitting the end punctuation marks. You may wish to add a box at the end of each sentence as shown below.

2. Photocopy the stories and give each child four stories (one for each side of the file folder).

3. Have the children glue one story to each side of the folder.

4. Laminate the folders for durability.

Directions:

Instruct each child to read the story on the folder, adding the correct punctuation with the wipe-off markers. When complete, the students can erase their work and exchange folders to try again. (**Note:** The work can be self-checked if you provide the books from which the pages are duplicated.)

What Is a Sentence?

Scrambled Sentences

Activity:

Students will play a game in small groups or as a center group activity in which they must unscramble words to make a sentence.

Materials:

- Scrambled Sentences Game Board (pages 27 and 28)
- game directions
- file folder
- colored pencils, crayons, or markers
- 1 die
- playing pieces

Preparation:

1. Program the blank game board with scrambled sentences the children will be able to read. (**Note:** If you wish to omit the text on the game board, white out the text before reproducing the pages.)

2. Color the game board.

3. Attach the completed game board to the inside of a file folder. Attach the directions to the back. Laminate the folder for durability.

4. Gather playing pieces and a die and store them with the game.

5. If desired, provide a list of the unscrambled sentences with the game board so that students can check themselves.

Directions:

Each group of students will choose a player to go first. Each player in turn rolls the die and moves ahead that number of spaces. The player must unscramble the sentence to stay on the space. Players who are unable to unscramble the sentence correctly must return to their previous locations.

What Is a Sentence?

Scrambled Sentences Game Board

Start

Move ahead 1 space.

Lose 1 turn.

Move back 1 space.

What Is a Sentence?

Scrambled Sentences Game Board *(cont.)*

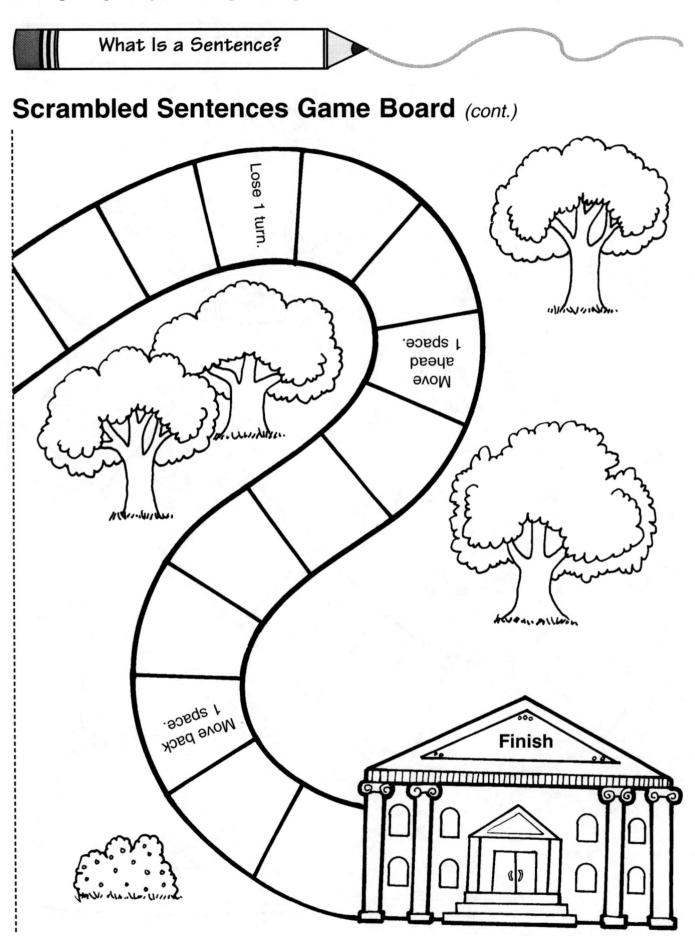

Lose 1 turn.

Move ahead 1 space.

Move back 1 space.

Finish

28

Retelling the Story

Activity:

The class will work together to retell a favorite tale in their own words.

Materials:

- storybook
- chart paper
- marking pen
- strips of sturdy paper or index cards (to be used for sentence strips in a pocket chart)
- pencils
- pocket chart

Preparation:

Prepare a title sentence strip for the story.

Directions:

Read the story to or with the children. Afterwards, have them review the story's events. As they state an event, record their responses on chart paper. (Be sure that they respond in complete sentences.)

Instruct each child to copy one response on a strip of paper, paying special attention to letter formation, the capital letter at the beginning of the sentence, and the punctuation at the end. Place the completed sentence strips in a pocket chart. Have the children check for capital letters at the beginning of all sentences and punctuation at the end.

As a class, place the sentences into the correct sequence and read in unison the story that has been composed.

Remove the sentence strips, stacking them in order. Add the previously prepared title sentence strip and staple all at the left side to form a class book.

The wolf said, "The better to hear you with, my dear."

Red Riding Hood's mother told her to go straight to Grandma's house.

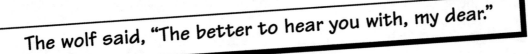

The wolf spied Red Riding Hood in the woods.

What Is a Sentence?

Put the Sentence Together

Activity:

Students work together as a class to build and read a sentence from a set of words.

Materials:

- sentence strips
- marking pen
- envelopes
- laminating machine
- scissors

Preparation:

1. Write a four- or five-word sentence on each sentence strip.
2. Laminate the strips.
3. Cut each strip apart into its individual words.
4. Put all the words for each sentence into an envelope.

Directions:

Divide the class into teams and give each team an envelope. (Place the same number of players on each team as their sentence has words.) Before the players open the envelopes, remind them of the clues to look for to find the first and last words of a sentence: a capital letter and an end punctuation mark.

To play, the teams take their words out and pass them around so that each teammate has a word. Each player then reads his or her word aloud to the rest of the team. The players arrange themselves in sentence order, lined up shoulder to shoulder, each holding his or her word so that the rest of the class can read it.

Call on each team, one at a time, to read the sentence for the class. When reading, each teammate will read his or her own word.

Note: As the children's skills improve, increase the length and difficulty of the sentences.

Teams can compete to form the sentence first, or they can compete against the clock.

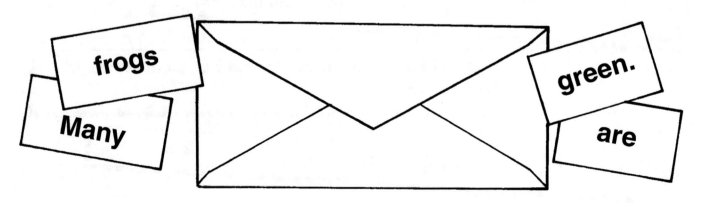

What I Made

Activity:

Students will write about an art project they have created.

Materials:

- previously made art project (1 per child)
- marking pen
- pencils
- chart paper
- writing paper

Preparation:

Prior to the lesson, have the children create an art project. These can be of an individual nature, or each child can add individual details to a teacher-determined art project.

Directions:

Use the art projects as the prewriting activity. Have the children brainstorm ways of describing their projects. Record their responses on chart paper.

Next, distribute writing paper and ask the children to write a topic sentence telling what they have made.

> **Example:** *I painted a jungle.*

Afterwards, instruct them to write three sentences that tell more about the project. Tell them to describe their work with more details.

> **Example:** *The trees in the jungle are green. A swinging monkey is in the tree. A yellow lion is walking in the jungle.*

Share the pictures and writing as a class. If desired, collect them into a class book to be displayed with the artwork.

Parts of Speech: Nouns

Noun Mobiles

Activity:

Students will identify nouns and work together to make noun mobiles.

Materials:

- 1 long strip of poster board per group of children
- 3 large pieces of construction paper per group of children
- marking pen
- yarn
- hole punch
- magazines
- scissors
- glue sticks

Preparation:

1. Label both sides of the poster board strips "Nouns." Label the top of both sides of each construction paper sheet with one of the following: "People," "Places," and "Things."

2. Punch a hole at the top of each construction paper card. Punch three holes across the bottom of the "Nouns" strip.

3. String yarn to each card and suspend each from the poster board strip by tying the yarn through a hole.

4. Punch a hole at the top of the noun strip and string yarn through it for later suspension. The mobile is now ready to be decorated by the students.

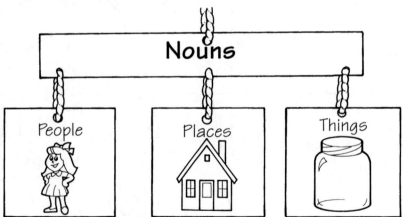

Directions:

Let the children know that a noun is a word that names a person, place, or thing. Some nouns mean one, and some nouns mean more than one. Some nouns name special people, places, or things, and these special nouns begin with a capital letter. After explaining the meaning of nouns, have the students brainstorm for words that fit the description.

Divide the students into groups. Give each group one of the mobiles you have made. Have the children work together to cut from magazines pictures that represent nouns and glue them onto both sides of the appropriate construction paper sheets.

When the mobiles are complete, display them for the students' reference.

Parts of Speech: Nouns

Labels, Labels, Labels

Activity:

Students will identify "nouns" in the room and label them.

Materials:

- index cards
- marking pen
- tape

Preparation:

No preparation is required.

Directions:

Review the definition of nouns with the children. When you feel they are ready, instruct them to look around the room to think of nouns, words that name things they see. Record the nouns they say, writing one noun per index card. Give at least one word to each child.

When you have gathered all the nouns you need, give one card to each child with a piece of tape. Instruct the students to tape their cards to the corresponding objects.

Leave the cards on display for awhile, allowing students to gain familiarity with the concept of nouns.

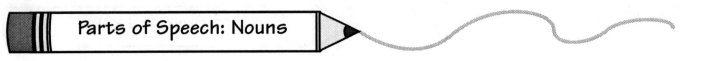

Parts of Speech: Nouns

Mural of Words

Activity:

Students will label nouns on a student-made mural.

Materials:

- large butcher paper
- markers
- crayons, markers, or paints
- label stickers

Preparation:

1. Choose an upcoming thematic unit of study.

2. Instruct the students to work as a class to create a mural under that theme. Everyone should have an opportunity to add to the mural. Be sure it includes plenty of detail. (**Note:** Brainstorming things the children already know about the theme or unit of study before beginning the mural will help you to develop the theme for study.)

Directions:

Display the completed mural. Ask the students to name the various items depicted. Write each item on a label. Have the students stick the labels to the mural in their correct places.

Keep the mural on display throughout your thematic unit. These labels can be used by the children when writing during the unit of study.

Note: Extend this activity with the exercise on page 52.

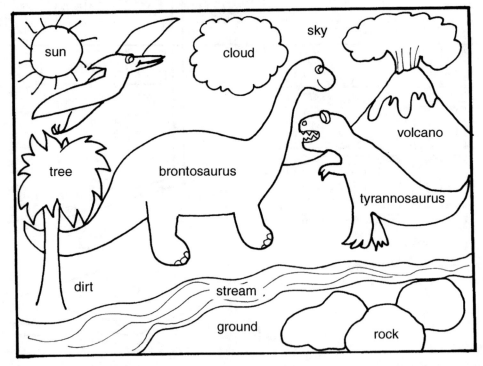

Parts of Speech: Nouns

Look and Locate

Activity:

Students will circle on a magazine page objects that represent nouns.

Materials:

- magazines
- markers or crayons

Preparation:

No preparation is required.

Directions:

Review the definition of a noun and give several examples. Ask the students to provide examples, as well.

Give each child a magazine. Have them open to any page and look for nouns. When they find a page they like, tear the page from the magazine. (You may wish to do this for them.) Instruct the children to write their names on the page.

Give each child a marker or crayon. Have them use the markers to circle all the nouns they find on their page. Stop them after five minutes. Allow each child to share the nouns he or she found. Make a list of the nouns on the chalkboard.

Note: This activity can be done with other parts of speech as well. The children can use the same page and look for more than one part of speech, using different colored markers or crayons to differentiate.

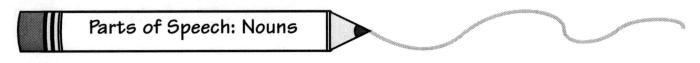

Parts of Speech: Nouns

Classify the Nouns

Activity:

Students will identify and classify the three types of nouns (people, places, and things) and use all three in a sentence.

Materials:

- magazines
- scissors
- index cards (3 per student)
- glue
- pencils
- writing paper

Preparation:

No preparation is required.

Directions:

There are three components to this activity. After reviewing the definition of a noun with the children, have each child find magazine pictures of a person, a place, and a thing. Instruct them to glue each picture to an index card.

When the picture cards are complete, collect and hold up each one. Have a child tell whether it is a picture of a person, a place, or a thing. If the answer is correct, ask the whole class to signal with a silent "thumbs-up," and if it is incorrect, ask them to silently signal "thumbs-down."

As each object is classified, place it in a pile with other people, places, and things. Then draw a card from each pile and model writing a sentence using all three nouns. Let the children follow suit, each child drawing a card from each stack and writing a sentence that uses all three nouns. Afterwards, allow them to share their sentences.

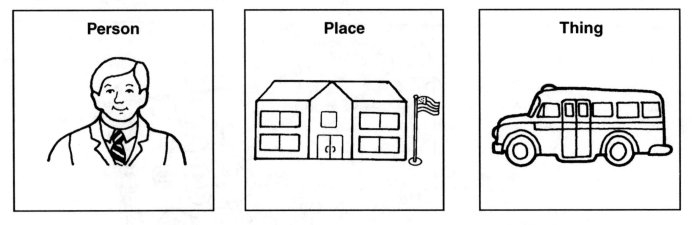

| Person | Place | Thing |

The teacher came to school on a bus.

Nuts About Nouns

Activity:

Students will write five nouns from each of three categories: people, places, and things.

Materials:

- 3 acorn patterns (below) per child
- scissors
- wipe-off markers
- marking pen
- laminating machine

Preparation:

1. For each child, use a marking to label one acorn "Things," another "Places," and the third "People."

2. Reproduce the labeled patterns, laminate them, and cut each acorn out.

Directions:

Give each child a set of three acorns, each with a different label. Using the wipe-off marker, the child writes five nouns for each category. When the sets are complete, allow the students to share with the class the nouns they have written.

1. _____
2. _____
3. _____
4. _____
5. _____

Parts of Speech: Nouns

Silly and Sensible Sentences

Activity:

Students will complete sentences with missing nouns and read the finished sentences.

Materials:

- small pictures of animals, food, people, vehicles, etc. (at least half as many as you have children)

- index cards (same number as you have pictures)

- sentence strips (at least half as many as you have children)

- pocket chart

- laminating machine (optional)

Preparation:

1. Mount each picture on a card.

2. Write a simple sentence about each picture on a sentence strip, leaving a blank space where the noun goes. (Example: To go with an apple picture, you might write, "An _____ is red and juicy.")

3. If desired, laminate the picture cards and sentence strips for durability.

Directions:

Review with the children the definition of a noun. Ask for examples of nouns to refresh their memories.

Next, model reading a sentence with a missing noun. Say the word "blank" when you come to the missing word. Have the students read a few such sentences with you.

Select a volunteer to choose a sentence strip and to read it first silently, then to read it aloud to the class, and finally to put it into the pocket chart.

Select another child to choose a picture to place in the blank of the sentence. The child may choose a picture that makes a silly sentence or a sensible one. He or she should say the name of the picture and then place it over the blank space in the sentence strip.

The class as a whole can read the complete sentence in unison as you point to the words. Repeat the whole process, choosing sentences and nouns until all children have had an opportunity to read and to select.

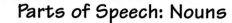

Parts of Speech: Nouns

Animal Bingo

Activity:

Students will play animal bingo, recognizing all animal names as nouns.

Materials:

- animal bingo cards (page 40)
- marking pen
- small pictures of animals, animal stickers, or animal rubber stamps and stamp pads
- corresponding large pictures of animals
- caller cards (page 41)
- construction paper
- scissors
- glue
- markers (corn kernels, beans, buttons, etc.)
- laminating machine (optional)

Preparation:

1. Copy a class set of bingo cards. Attach or draw pictures of animals and print the animal's name in each of the empty squares of the bingo cards, creating a different card for each child. Attach the completed bingo cards to construction paper for stability. Laminate them, if desired.

2. Copy the required number of caller cards so that you have a square for every animal pictured on the bingo cards. Attach or draw a picture of each animal used on the bingo cards to a caller card. Attach the completed cards to construction paper and laminate them, if desired.

3. Glue the large pictures to construction paper for stability. Laminate them, if desired.

Directions:

Provide each player with a bingo card and a number of markers. Let the children know that the name of every animal on the cards is a noun.

Select one child to be the "caller." The caller draws and holds up a large picture card and says the name of the animal. Each player places a marker on every animal called that is on his or her bingo card. The caller marks the animal on his or her cards as well so that there is a record of all animals called.

Players may win with three-in-a-row, with the four corners, or by blackout.

Note: Once the children know how to play the game, it can become a small group or center activity.

Parts of Speech: Nouns

Animal Bingo Cards

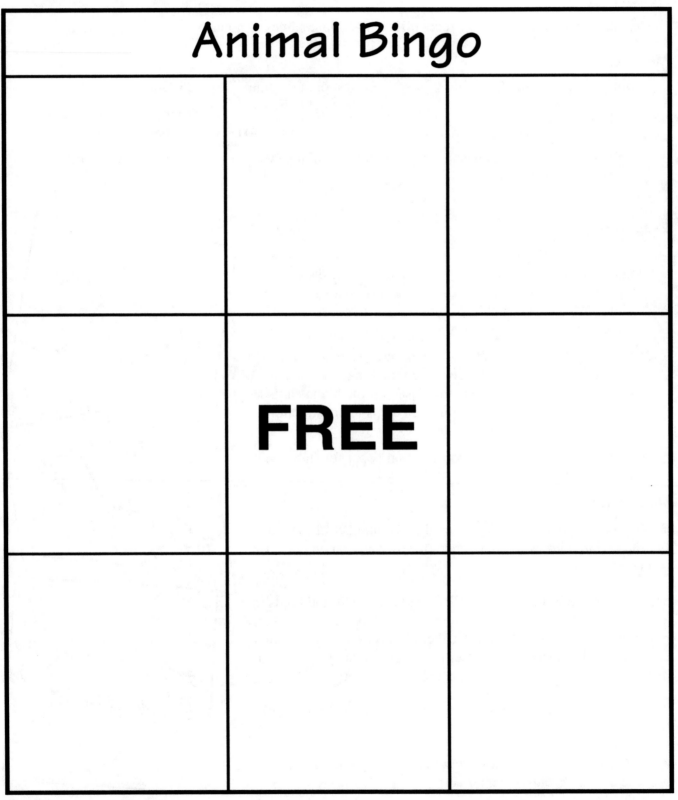

Parts of Speech: Nouns

Animal Bingo Caller Cards

Parts of Speech: Nouns

Balloon Basketball

Activity:

Students will identify nouns as belonging to the person, place, or thing category.

Materials:

- 3 poster boards
- 6 large boxes, baskets, or tubs
- permanent marking pen
- balloons (more than 1 per student)

Preparation:

1. Use the poster board to make three large signs, each one labelled one of the following: People, Places, and Things.

2. Inflate the balloons.

3. Write a noun on each balloon with a permanent maker. If you wish, make some pictures on the balloons to match the nouns.

4. Divide the balloons among three boxes.

5. Attach the poster board signs to each of the three remaining boxes so that they can be easily seen.

Directions:

Place the labelled boxes in a row. Place the balloon boxes in a row two or three feet (one meter) away from the first row. Divide the students into three teams, lining up each team behind a box of balloons.

The object of the game is to empty the balloon box by placing the balloons into the boxes with the corresponding signs. For example, if a balloon reads "flower," it should be placed in the "Things" box.

At your signal the first child on each team chooses a balloon, reads the noun, runs to the correct box, places the balloon in it, and then stands behind the box in which he or she has placed the balloon. When he or she has finished, the next student in line grabs a balloon and follows the same procedure.

Play continues in this manner until all players from a team are lined up behind the noun boxes. If desired, pull the balloons out of the boxes and as a class determine if they have been placed correctly.

Parts of Speech: Nouns

Dyno Detective

Activity:

Students will become "detectives" to locate nouns and other parts of speech.

Materials:

- Dyno Detective Notebook Cover (1 per child, page 44)
- Dyno Detective Poster (page 45)
- Dyno Detective Task Cards (pages 46-48)
- Dyno Detective Awards (page 49)
- marking pen
- construction paper
- writing paper

- stapler
- crayons, markers, or colored pencils
- paper clip
- scissors
- pencils
- laminating machine (optional)

Preparation:

1. Make Dyno Detective notebooks. To do so, duplicate the notebook cover (page 44) onto construction paper, filling in your room number in the blank at the bottom. Cut same-sized covers from construction paper (these will be the back covers). Cut a supply of writing paper to fit between the covers, and staple everything together. There should be one notebook per student.

2. Reproduce the Dyno Detective Poster (page 45). Write your room number in the correct blank. Color the poster and mount it on construction paper. Laminate it, if desired. Make a slit along the dotted line in the Dyno Detective Special Task box. Slip a paper clip through the slit from the back.

3. Copy, laminate, and cut out the noun task cards (page 46). Save the cards on page 47 for when you study verbs. The cards on page 48 can be filled in at your discretion for additional noun and verb investigations or for other parts of speech.

4. Copy and cut out the Dyno Detective Awards (page 49).

Directions:

This is an ongoing activity that "investigates" nouns and other parts of speech. You will need to decide on the frequency of your investigative sessions as well as their length of time.

Display the Dyno Detective Poster for a few days to pique the children's curiosity. Then gather the children to pass out their Dyno Detective notebooks and to explain the detective process. (Allow the students to write their names on the covers.) Let the students know that a different task card will be inserted in the poster's Special Task section during each detective-work period. Then, choose a task card and attach it to the Dyno Detective Poster. Work with the students to complete this first investigation. Afterwards, let them do their detective work individually or with a partner.

Share the children's investigative work at the end of the allotted time.

Parts of Speech: Nouns

Dyno Detective Notebook Cover

Dyno Detective!

Detective

_____

Working for Room _____ Investigations

Parts of Speech: Nouns

Dyno Detective Poster

Be a Dyno Detective!

Here is today's Dyno Detective task.

- **Jot down your information carefully.**

- **Keep your eyes and ears open!**

Special Task

Room _____ Investigations

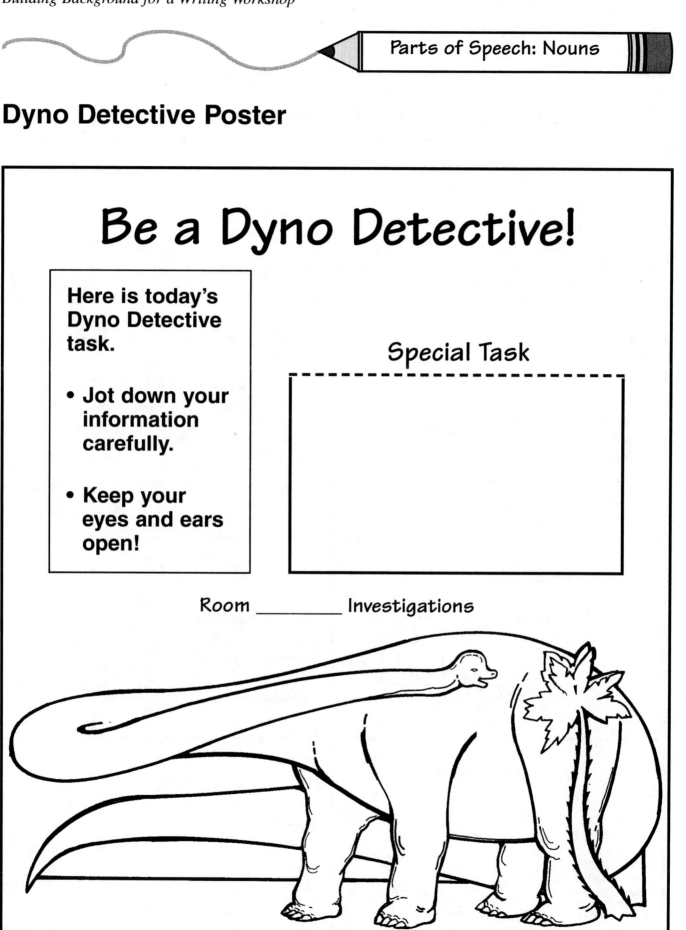

Parts of Speech: Nouns

Dyno Detective Task Cards: Nouns

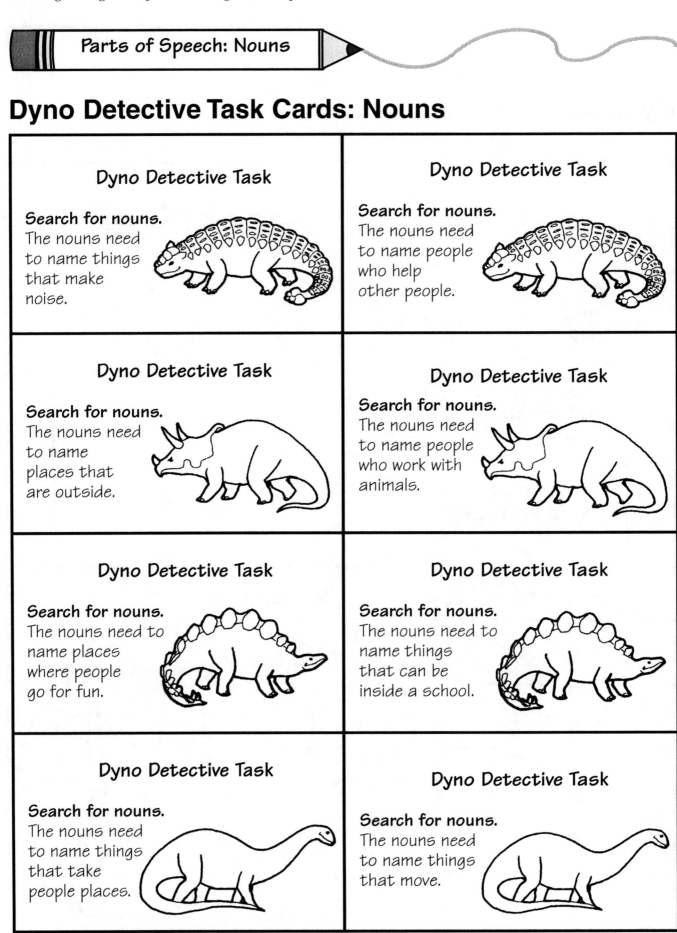

Dyno Detective Task

Search for nouns.
The nouns need
to name things
that make
noise.

Dyno Detective Task

Search for nouns.
The nouns need
to name people
who help
other people.

Dyno Detective Task

Search for nouns.
The nouns need
to name
places that
are outside.

Dyno Detective Task

Search for nouns.
The nouns need
to name people
who work with
animals.

Dyno Detective Task

Search for nouns.
The nouns need to
name places
where people
go for fun.

Dyno Detective Task

Search for nouns.
The nouns need to
name things
that can be
inside a school.

Dyno Detective Task

Search for nouns.
The nouns need
to name things
that take
people places.

Dyno Detective Task

Search for nouns.
The nouns need
to name things
that move.

Dyno Detective Task Cards: Verbs

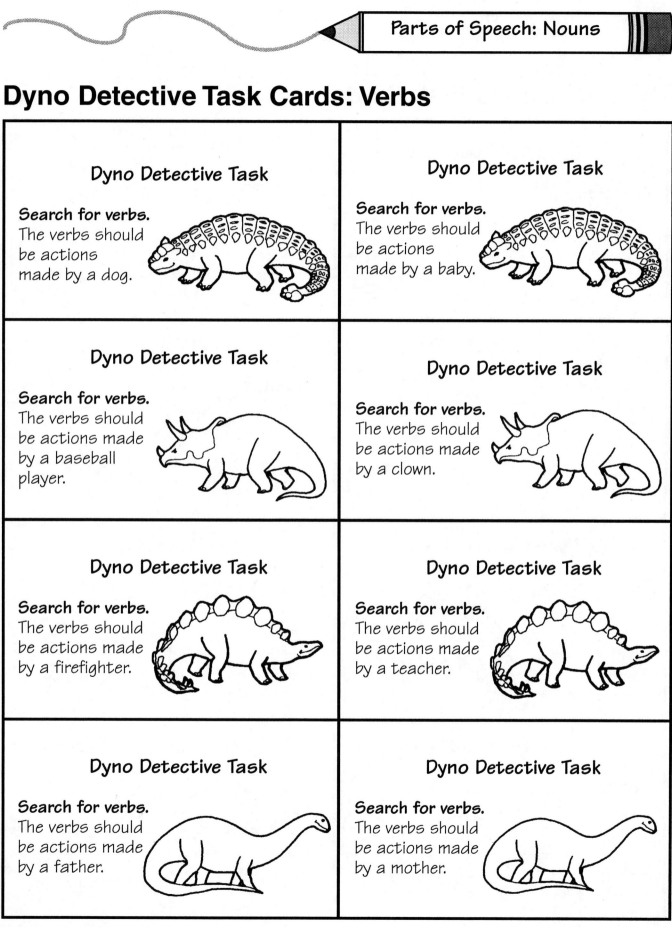

Dyno Detective Task

Search for verbs.
The verbs should
be actions
made by a dog.

Dyno Detective Task

Search for verbs.
The verbs should
be actions
made by a baby.

Dyno Detective Task

Search for verbs.
The verbs should
be actions made
by a baseball
player.

Dyno Detective Task

Search for verbs.
The verbs should
be actions made
by a clown.

Dyno Detective Task

Search for verbs.
The verbs should
be actions made
by a firefighter.

Dyno Detective Task

Search for verbs.
The verbs should
be actions made
by a teacher.

Dyno Detective Task

Search for verbs.
The verbs should
be actions made
by a father.

Dyno Detective Task

Search for verbs.
The verbs should
be actions made
by a mother.

Parts of Speech: Nouns

Dyno Detective Task Cards

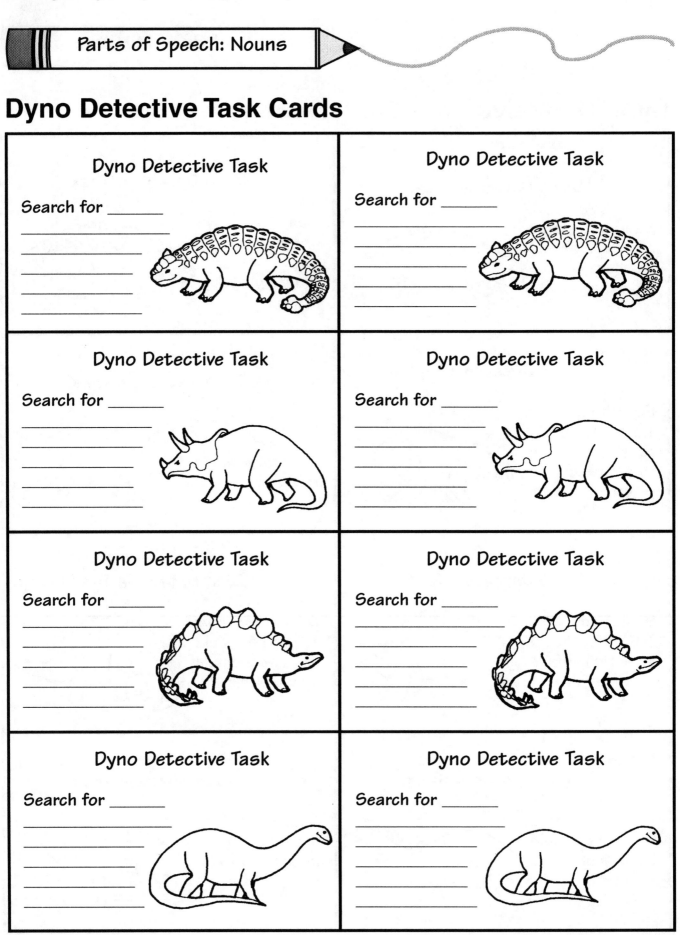

Dyno Detective Task

Search for _____

_____

_____

_____

_____

Dyno Detective Task

Search for _____

_____

_____

_____

_____

Dyno Detective Task

Search for _____

_____

_____

_____

_____

Dyno Detective Task

Search for _____

_____

_____

_____

_____

Dyno Detective Task

Search for _____

_____

_____

_____

_____

Dyno Detective Task

Search for _____

_____

_____

_____

_____

Dyno Detective Task

Search for _____

_____

_____

_____

_____

Dyno Detective Task

Search for _____

_____

_____

_____

_____

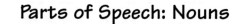

Parts of Speech: Nouns

Dyno Detective Awards

Detective _____

is

hot

on

the

trail

of

_____

_____

Congratulations!

_____

solved the case!

What a Dyno-mite Detective!

Top Secret!

_____

is a Dyno-mite Detective!

Detective _____

is a

Dyno-mite

Detective

when it

comes to

_____

_____

Keep up the great work!

Parts of Speech: Verbs

Identifying Action Verbs

Activity:

Students will identify action verbs and work together to make verb mobiles.

Materials:

- 1 long strip of poster board per group of children
- 3 large pieces of construction paper per group of children
- hole punch
- scissors
- marking pen
- yarn
- magazines
- glue sticks

Preparation:

1. Label both sides of the poster board strips "Verbs." Label the top of both sides of each construction paper sheet "Actions."

2. Punch a hole at the top of each construction paper card. Punch three holes across the bottom of the "verb" strip.

3. String yarn to each card and suspend each from the poster board strip by tying the yarn through a hole.

4. Punch a hole at the top of the verb strip and string yarn through it for later suspension. The mobile is now ready to be decorated by the students.

Directions:

Let the children know that a verb is a word that names an action. Some verbs tell what people and animals do. Some verbs tell about more than one action. After explaining the meaning of verbs, have the students brainstorm for words that fit the description.

Divide the students into groups. Give each group one of the mobiles you have made. Have the children work together to cut from magazines pictures that represent verbs (show an action) and glue them onto both sides of the construction paper sheets.

When they are complete, display the mobiles for the students' reference. Laminate the picture cards, if desired.

Note: If poster board is unavailable, use a hanger and tape or tie verb signs on it. Then, string the "actions" signs to the bottom of the hanger.

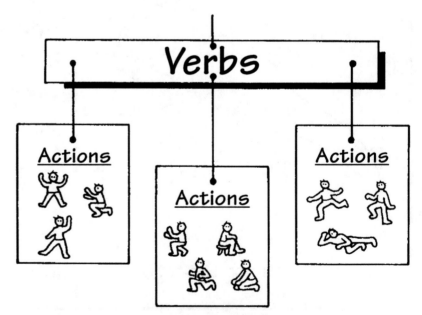

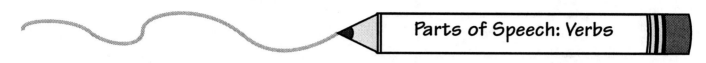

All the Right Moves

Activity:

Students will identify and pantomime action verbs and then find verbs within sentences.

Materials:

- chalkboard or overhead projector
- chart paper
- marker
- large open area such as a gym or playground
- sentence strips
- laminating machine (optional)

Preparation:

On the chalkboard or an overhead projector, write several sample sentences which contain easily identifiable action verbs.

Directions:

After a brief discussion about motion and movement, have the children brainstorm different actions (verbs). Write their ideas on chart paper.

Take the children and the list of verbs to an open area such as the playground or gymnasium. Instruct the children to act out selected verbs from the list.

Back in the classroom, ask the children to identify the verbs in the previously prepared sentences. The sentences can then be copied onto sentence strips, laminated (if desired), and placed in a center to reinforce the students' ability to identify action verbs.

Verbs
Mary jumps rope.
Sammy runs fast.
hops   skips
walks   runs
gallops   jogs

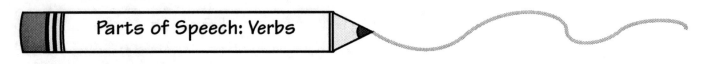

Parts of Speech: Verbs

Mural of Verbs

Activity:

Students will label verbs on a self-made mural.

Materials:

- markers
- label stickers
- Mural of Words (page 34)

Preparation:

Display the mural made previously when studying nouns (page 34).

Directions:

Review with the students the labelled nouns on the thematic mural. Instruct the children to add action verbs on labels under the nouns. These verbs should indicate methods of movement for each noun.

These nouns and verbs can also be used by the children when writing about the unit of study.

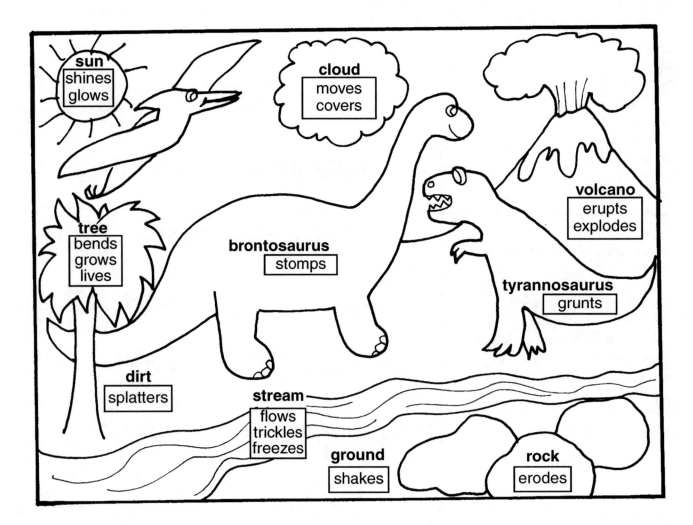

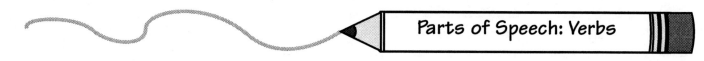

Parts of Speech: Verbs

Topic Poems

Activity:

Students will list nouns and gerund verbs under a topic and create a poem that incorporates them.

Materials:

- chart paper
- pencils
- white paper (larger than writing paper)
- marker
- glue
- writing paper
- crayons

Preparation:

Select a topic.

Directions:

Introduce the topic to the children and ask them to brainstorm for nouns that relate to it. Next have them brainstorm for verbs that relate to the topic and the nouns, adding "ing" to each to make the gerund form. As the students brainstorm, list their ideas in two columns like these:

Topic: school		A Day of School
Nouns	**Verbs**	*Teacher teaching,*
teacher	teaching	*Principal talking,*
librarian	reading	*Librarian reading,*
children	working	*Children working,*
piano	playing	*Pencil writing,*
pencil	writing	*Crayon coloring,*
crayon	coloring	*Paint painting,*
paint	painting	*All in a day of school.*
balls	bouncing	
principal	talking	

Select seven noun-verb pairs from your lists, making a series of phrases about the topic. Construct the phrases into a poem for the students, adding a final sentence that summarizes the topic. (A sample poem, created from the nouns and verbs lists, is provided on the right.)

Now, send the children off to write poems of their own under a different topic. Once they have completed their poems, glue each to a large sheet of construction paper and let students add art in the borders or in the space above or below the poem.

Note: Practice makes perfect! This is an enjoyable activity that becomes easier the more it is practiced, and it is appropriate for numerous topics.

Parts of Speech: Verbs

Action Alphabet Class Book

Activity:

The class will make an alphabet book of verbs.

Materials:

- chart paper
- large pieces of construction paper (1 per child)
- stapler, hole punch and yarn, or hole punch and binding rings

- marker
- poster board
- crayons

Preparation:

1. List the alphabet letters on the chart paper, leaving space to the right of each to list words.

2. Make a front and back cover for the class book from poster board. Title ideas include "The Action Alphabet," "First Grade's Action Alphabet," and "Room 10's Action Alphabet."

Directions:

Review verbs with the children. Have the children brainstorm a list of action words, one or more per alphabet letter. Record the verbs next to the appropriate letter on the chart paper.

Allow each child to choose a letter and a corresponding verb from the list. The children will each make a page for the class book, using construction paper. Each page should contain the following:

- the alphabet letter
- the verb
- an illustration

Depending on the developmental level of the children, a sentence which includes the verb can be written on each page.

Bind the completed pages and the cover to make a class book.

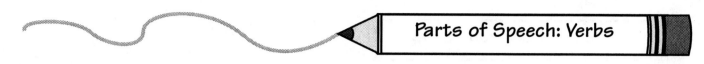

Parts of Speech: Verbs

Presto-Chango Verbs

Activity:

Students will give new meanings to sentences by changing the verbs.

Materials:

- reading textbook or storybook

Preparation:

Select several simple sentences from the book, each with an action verb.

Directions:

Have a child read a selected sentence and identify the action verb. Ask another child to read the same sentence, changing the verb to a different one that makes sense. Then, allow a third child to change the verb again and so on, for example:

Child 1: "The ant tunnelled under the rock."

Child 2: "The ant read under the rock."

Child 3: "The ant slept under the rock."

Continue until the class can think of no more appropriate verbs. Then begin again with another sentence.

Parts of Speech: Verbs

Animal Action Class Book

Activity:

The class will make a book of animals and their actions.

Materials:

- chart paper
- poster board
- markers
- large pieces of construction paper (1 per child)
- laminating machine (optional)
- stapler, hole punch, and yarn or hole punch and binding rings

Preparation:

Make a front and back cover for the class book from poster board. If desired, laminate the covers for durability. A suggested title for the book is "Animal Actions."

Directions:

Review the definition of verbs with the children. Then ask them to brainstorm for a list of animals and the ways in which they move. Record their ideas (both the animals and the action verbs) on chart paper.

Next, have each child choose an animal and a verb from the list and create a page for the class book on a large piece of construction paper. Each page should contain the following:

- the animal's name
- the verb
- an illustration of the animal moving

Depending on the developmental level of the children, a sentence which includes the animal's name and the verb can be written on each page. Bind the completed pages and the cover to make a class book.

56

Parts of Speech: Verbs

Hot, Hot, Hot

Activity:

Students will name verbs and nouns and use them in sentences.

Materials :

- 2 different-colored balls
- chart paper and marker or chalkboard
- permanent marking pen
- music and music player

Preparation:

Label one ball "noun" and the other "verb."

Directions:

Hot, Hot, Hot is a version of the game Hot Potato. The children sit in a circle and pass the two balls as the music plays. When the music stops, each child with a ball names a word that corresponds with the part of speech listed on the ball being held. The other children give a silent signal (thumbs-up) if correct. If the word is correct, the child holding the ball uses the given word in a sentence. If it is incorrect, the child tries again.

After both children have given a sentence, the music starts and play continues. Encourage each child to use a different noun and verb by charting each child's response.

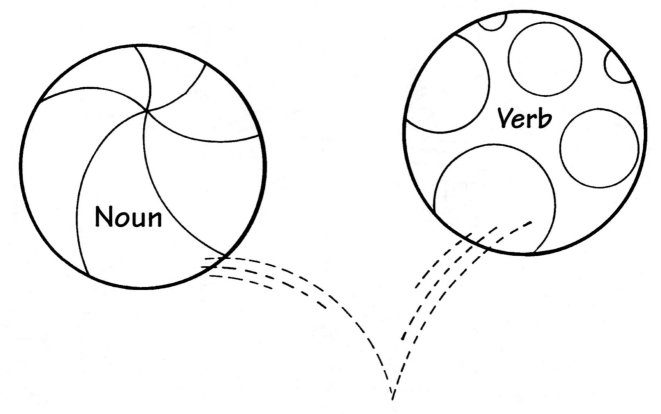

Parts of Speech: Verbs

Parts of Speech Sort

Activity:

Students will sort words into nouns and verbs.

Materials:

- 3 baskets or boxes (or more, if you have studied additional parts of speech)
- index cards
- marking pens
- tape
- laminating machine (optional)

Preparation:

1. Write a noun or verb (and any other part of speech you have already taught) on each small card.

2. If you wish to keep the cards for use in future years, laminate them for durability.

3. Place the cards in a large box so they can be sorted.

4. Make a part-of-speech label for each box and tape it to the box. At the minimum, you will need a nouns label and a verbs label.

Directions:

This activity is best done at a center. Instruct the students to read the word on each card and then to place each card in the correct box.

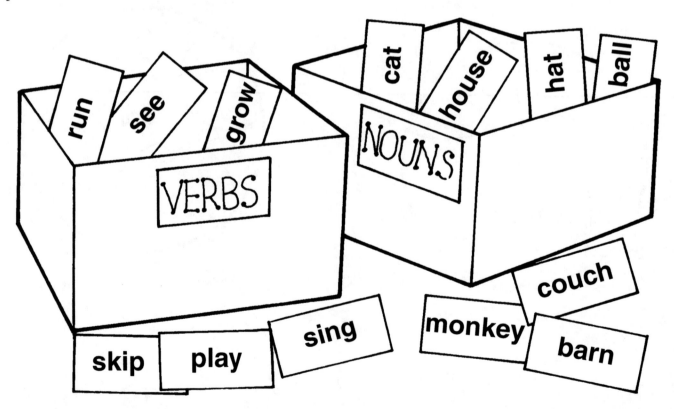

Parts of Speech: Verbs

Sammy Says Verbs

Activity:

Students will move in response to hearing a verb.

Materials:

- list of verbs
- marking pen
- large area in which to stand and move
- index cards
- basket or box

Preparation:

1. Together with the students, brainstorm a list of action verbs. Do these several days prior to the activity to create some distance between the list and the activity.

2. Write each verb on the list on an index card.

3. Write several other words (nouns, adjectives, etc.) on additional cards.

4. Place all the cards in the basket or box.

Directions:

Sammy Says Verbs is played just like the familiar game Simon Says. Ask the children to stand. Choose one to be "Sammy." Sammy draws a card from the basket and says, "Sammy says . . . ," adding the word at the end. If Sammy says a word that is not a verb, the children stand still, but if Sammy says a verb, the children should pantomime the action. Children who make a mistake take their seats. The last child standing becomes the next Sammy, if you wish to continue play. As an alternative, you can choose a different Sammy each time a word is drawn. Simply let that Sammy rejoin the group afterwards.

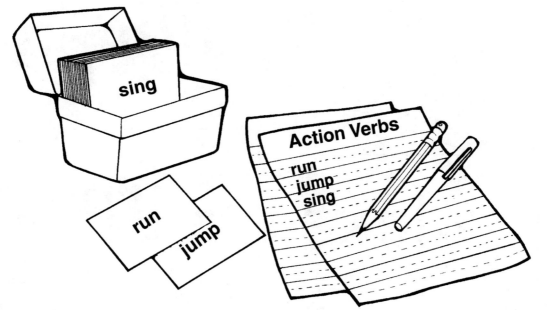

Parts of Speech: Verbs

Matchmaker

Activity:

Students will pair action verbs with subject nouns.

Materials:

- Matchmaker Cards (pages 61 and 62)
- scissors
- laminating machine (optional)
- crayons, markers, or colored pencils
- 2 self-sealing bags

Preparation:

1. Color and laminate (if desired) the noun pictures and verb cards. Cut them out.

2. Place the noun picture cards in one bag and the verb cards in another. Label the bags "nouns" and "verbs."

Directions:

Instruct the students to choose a verb from the verb bag. They should then find as many noun pictures to match that verb as they can. All chosen pictures and verbs should make sense when placed together. This is an excellent center activity.

To extend the activity, ask the students to create additional cards to challenge their classmates. You can also have the students write sentences for some of the matches. Post their sentences to see how many different concepts can come from the same subject noun and verb.

Parts of Speech: Verbs

Matchmaker Cards

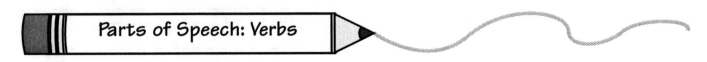

Parts of Speech: Verbs

Matchmaker Cards *(cont.)*

squeaks	**swims**	**waves**
tickles	**grows**	**sings**
flies	**runs**	**burns**
stands	**hatches**	**bounces**
crawls	**blows**	**barks**
opens	**smiles**	**throws**
eats	**sits**	**falls**

Parts of Speech: Verbs

Sentence Building

Activity:

Students will locate one or more verbs and/or one or more nouns and use them in a sentence.

Materials:

- task cards (page 64)
- glue
- scissors
- writing paper
- magazines and newspapers

Preparation:

Copy the task cards and laminate them for durability.

Directions:

A child selects a task card. Using the magazines and newspapers, the child locates the requested word or words and then completes the task. Their sentences can be written on the writing paper, and they can glue the preprinted word or words in the correct place in the sentence.

If desired, have each child complete more than one task card or have the students work in small groups or with partners. Create additional task cards, as needed.

This activity can be used to evaluate both the child's understanding of nouns and verbs as well his or her understanding of a complete sentence.

Parts of Speech: Verbs

Sentence Building Task Cards

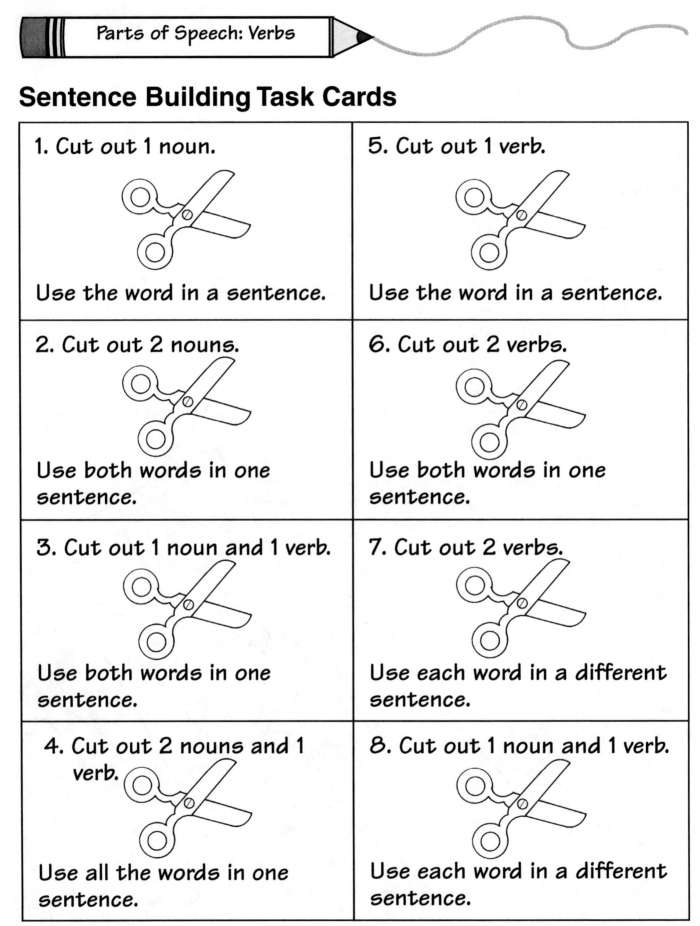

1. Cut out 1 noun.

Use the word in a sentence.

2. Cut out 2 nouns.

Use both words in one sentence.

3. Cut out 1 noun and 1 verb.

Use both words in one sentence.

4. Cut out 2 nouns and 1 verb.

Use all the words in one sentence.

5. Cut out 1 verb.

Use the word in a sentence.

6. Cut out 2 verbs.

Use both words in one sentence.

7. Cut out 2 verbs.

Use each word in a different sentence.

8. Cut out 1 noun and 1 verb.

Use each word in a different sentence.

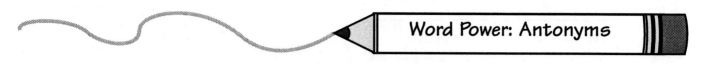

Word Power: Antonyms

Opposites

Activity:

Students will find and list antonyms.

Materials:

- children's book about opposites (such as *Inside, Outside, Upside Down* by Stan and Janice Berenstain)
- chart paper
- marking pen
- Opposites Brainstorming Sheet (page 66, 1 per group)
- pencils

Preparation:

1. Read aloud the children's book about opposites.

2. Use the word *antonyms* and discuss the definition with the children. Antonyms are words that have opposite meanings.

Directions:

Partner the children and give each team a brainstorming sheet. Instruct each team to brainstorm a list of words with opposite meanings. Stop the children after five minutes. Use the chart paper to record a compiled list of the antonyms they have found. Post the list for the children's reference.

Periodically review the list and add any new antonyms the children have learned.

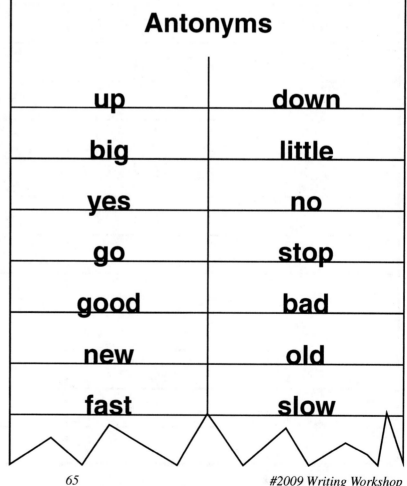

Antonyms	
up	down
big	little
yes	no
go	stop
good	bad
new	old
fast	slow

Word Power: Antonyms

Opposites Brainstorming Sheet

Opposites (Antonyms)	
Write the word here.	**Write the opposite (antonym) here.**

Word Power: Antonyms

Antonyms Leaves

Activity:

Students will match sets of antonyms.

Materials:

- multiple copies of the leaf pattern
- marking pen
- colored pencils, markers, or crayons
- laminating machine (optional)

Preparation:

1. Copy and cut out five leaves per child.

2. Lightly color the leaves and cut them out. (To save time, you may wish to reproduce the pattern on lightly-colored paper.)

3. Cut the leaves in half, forming two puzzle pieces each.

4. Write one word from a pair of opposites on each piece of a leaf puzzle. If desired, laminate the puzzle pieces for durability.

Directions:

Instruct the students to read the words on the leaf pieces and to put the leaf puzzles together by matching the antonyms.

Note: Other seasonal or thematic shapes can be used for this activity, as well. Also, this makes an excellent center activity.

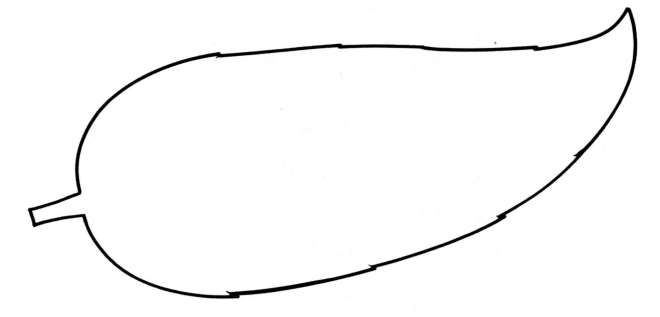

Word Power: Antonyms

Card Cube

Activity:

Student teams will match pairs of antonyms.

Materials:

- index cards
- marking pen

- Antonym Word List (page 69)
- empty square tissue box

Preparation:

1. Label an even number of index cards with antonyms, one word per card.
2. Label the outside of the tissue box "Antonyms."
3. Remove the plastic insert in the opening of the box.
4. Place the cards inside the opening of the box.

Directions:

Two students can play at a time. Each child draws a card from the cube. If the cards match, they set them aside and each draws another card. If the cards do not match, both cards are put back into the cube and play continues. When all the cards have been matched, the game is over.

This is a very versatile game. It can be played to match synonyms, contractions, compound words, and many more. Anything that can be paired can be reviewed with this activity.

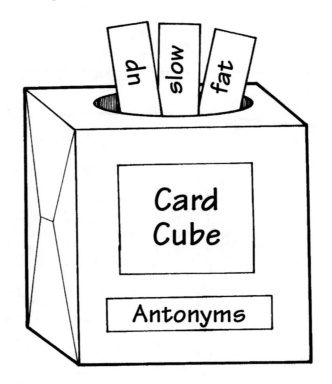

Word Power: Antonyms

Antonym Word List

The following antonyms are appropriate for study in the primary grades. Use them for the Card Cube and other antonym activities as desired.

aunt - uncle	happy - sad
back - front	hard - soft
good - bad	heavy - light
big - little	high - low
black - white	huge - tiny
boy - girl	in - out
brother - sister	large - small
clean - dirty	left - right
come - go	long - short
cold - hot	loose - tight
close - open	lose - win
dark - light	mine - yours
daughter - son	new - old
down - up	night - day
dry - wet	noisy - quiet
fast - slow	off - on
fat - thin	old - young
father - mother	over - under
float - sink	pretty - ugly
from - to	right - wrong
give - take	rough - smooth
go - stop	short - tall

Word Power: Homophones

They Sound the Same

Activity:

Students will brainstorm a list of homophones and use them in sentences.

Materials:

- *Eye Spy: A Mysterious Alphabet* by Linda Bourke
- chart paper
- marking pen

Preparation:

No preparation is required.

Directions:

Homophones are words that sound the same but have different meanings and spellings. Use the word *homophones* and discuss the definition with the children. Then read *Eye Spy: A Mysterious Alphabet* by Linda Bourke or another book that uses homophones. The reading will help to reinforce the concept.

Ask the students to name some homophone pairs. Use the chart paper to record a list of the homophones, leaving space after each one and grouping the pairs by leaving space between the sets. After listing those the children know, add additional sets that are familiar to the students. (A partial list of homophones is provided on page 73.)

Once your list is complete, begin with the first set of homophones on the list and ask a child to use one of the words in a sentence. Write the sentence next to the word. Then ask another child to give a sentence for the other word, and write that sentence in its appropriate place. If the students can not suggest a sentence, it is likely they do not know the meaning of the word. This is a "teaching moment"—use it!

Keep the list of homophones and sentences for the children's future reference. Periodically review the list and add any new homophones the children have learned and are using.

Homophones
ant–The ant ate the cracker crumb.
aunt–My aunt gave me a new bike.
bee–The bee stung me.
be–I want to be a ghost for Halloween.
two–The two dogs chased each other.
to–I will go to the park.
too–I want to go, too.

Word Power: Homophones

Which Witch?

Activity:

Students will place homophones in prewritten sentences.

Materials:

- sentence strips
- marking pen
- They Sound the Same sentences (page 70)
- witch pattern (below)
- pocket chart
- laminating machine (optional)

Preparation:

1. Write the sentences on sentence strips, leaving a blank space for the homophone.

2. Photocopy one witch pattern for each homophone and cut it out.

3. Write one homophone on each witch.

4. Laminate the witches for durability, if desired.

5. Place the sentences in the pocket chart.

Directions:

Read a sentence aloud. Ask a student to choose the witch that fits in the sentence and to place it in the blank space. Let the class give a silent thumbs-up if correct. Read another sentence and select another student. Continue until all the witches have been placed appropriately.

Note: Other seasonal or thematic shapes can be used for this activity, as well.

Word Power: Homophones

Homophone Dominoes

Activity :

Students will match homophones, using domino style.

Materials:

- ruler
- marking pen
- small rectangular cards for dominoes (15 pieces per partner group)
- laminating machine (optional)

Preparation:

1. Draw a line in the middle of each small card to form a domino.

2. Write one word from a set of homophones on each side of a domino. Be careful not to put a matching homophone pair on any one domino.

3. If preparing more than one set of dominoes, use different-colored markers to write the words so they will be easy to sort. Or if using cardstock, use different-color stock to differentiate.

4. Laminate dominoes for durability, if desired.

Directions:

Place all dominoes in a stack upside down. Divide the students into partners. Each player draws five dominoes, concealing them from his or her partner. One domino from the remaining upside-down pile is turned up to start play.

Player number 1 tries to match one of the words on the domino with its homophone from his or her own pile. If player 1 has a match, he or she places it perpendicularly next to the first domino. If the player does not have a homophone match, that player draws from the upside-down pile until one is found.

Play continues until one of the players is out of dominoes and there are no more from which to draw.

to	be	bee

	ant	aunt	not

			knot

four	for	whole	hole

night

Word Power: Homophones

Homophone Word List

The following homophones are appropriate for study in the primary grades. Use them for these or other homophone activities, as desired.

ant - aunt	meat - meet
ate - eight	night - knight
be - bee	one - won
buy - by	peace - piece
capital - capitol	plain - plane
cent - sent	principal - principle
sight - site	rain - reign
dear - deer	right - write
do - due	road - rode
flea - flee	role - roll
flew - flu	sail - sale
for - four	sea - see
heal - heel	some - sum
hear - here	son - sun
hole - whole	tail - tale
hour - our	toe - tow
in - inn	their - there - they're
knew - new	to - too - two
knot - not	weak - week
mail - male	wood - would

Word Power: Synonyms

Almost the Same

Activity:

Students will match words to their synonyms.

Materials:

- list of synonyms (page 77)
- chart paper
- tape
- marking pen
- index cards

Preparation

1. Select as many pairs of synonyms as there are students in your class.

2. Write one word from each synonym pair on an index card.

3. List the synonyms of the previous words on chart paper, leaving space next to each for the index cards to be placed.

Directions:

Use the word synonym and discuss its definition with the children. Synonyms are words which have the same or nearly the same meaning. Encourage the children to think of and share any synonyms they know.

Read the list of synonyms to the students. Pass out an index card to each child and ask the students to silently read their cards. Then give each child a piece of tape to form into a ring (sticky side out) to attach to the back of the card. One at a time, ask the children to read the words on their cards to the class and then to attach them to the chart next to their synonyms.

Ask the class to give the silent signal (thumbs-up or thumbs-down) as an assessment. Allow any child who does not choose the correct synonym match to make the correction.

Post the synonym chart for the students' future reference. Periodically review the list, adding new synonyms when appropriate.

Synonyms

thin   slim

fast   rapid

pretty

journey

slow

Word Power: Synonyms

Pair Them Up

Activity:

Students will match synonym pairs.

Materials:

- shoe pattern below (10 per set)
- colored pencils, markers, or crayons
- marking pen
- laminating machine (optional)

Preparation:

1. Reproduce, color, and cut out the shoe shape as many times as necessary.

2. Write one synonym on each shoe, making five pairs for each student group or each student working at a center.

3. Laminate for durability, if desired.

4. Store each set of tennis shoes in a different shoebox.

Directions:

Instruct the students to read the word on each shoe. Students can match the shoe pairs by placing the synonym shoes on top of one another.

Note: Other skills such as compound words and contractions can be reviewed in this way.

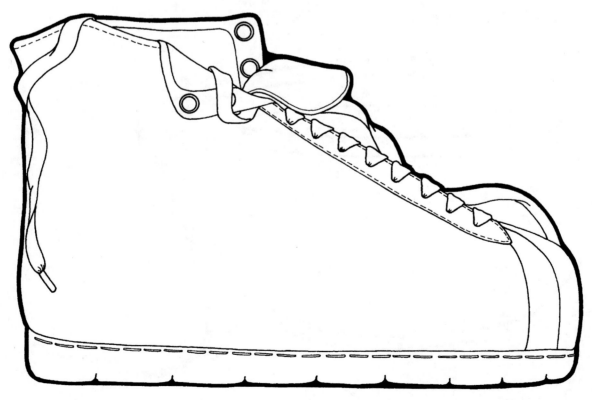

Word Power: Synonyms

Thesaurus Sundae

Activity:

Students will find and write synonyms for given words, using a thesaurus.

Materials:

- index cards
- marking pen
- box or bag
- bowl pattern (1 per student or group)
- ice cream scoop pattern (several per student or group)
- glue
- pencils
- thesauri

Preparation:

1. Make a list of commonly used adjectives such as good, fun, pretty, nice, and so forth.

2. Write each word on an index card.

3. Place the cards in the box or bag.

Directions:

Have the students work individually or in groups. Instruct each individual or group to draw a card from the box. They are then to use a thesaurus and their own knowledge to find as many synonyms for the word as they can. Each synonym should be written on an ice-cream scoop. The scoops can be glued together "in" the bowl and the original word written on the bowl. Display the thesaurus sundaes on a bulletin board for future student reference.

76

Word Power: Synonyms

Synonym Word List

The following synonyms are appropriate for study in the primary grades. Use them for these or other synonym activities, as desired.

afraid	scared	frightened	terrified
angry	mad	furious	irritated
bad	wicked	evil	harmful
beautiful	cute	lovely	pretty
big	gigantic	huge	enormous
brave	courageous	fearless	bold
fast	hasty	rapid	speedy
fat	big	plump	stout
fight	argue	quarrel	disagree
funny	amusing	witty	humorous
give	offer	grant	award
good	worthy	pure	upright
good	skillful	expert	clever
great	fabulous	majestic	stately
grouchy	cross	disagreeable	cranky
grow	sprout	expand	increase
happy	joyous	glad	merry
journey	tour	trip	voyage
miserable	sad	unhappy	depressed
mistake	error	slip	blunder
person	human	individual	character
say	declare	state	express
sick	ill	unhealthy	unwell
silly	foolish	stupid	senseless
skinny	slender	slim	thin
slow	dragging	sluggish	leisurely
smart	clever	intelligent	wise
sparkling	gleaming	glistening	glittering
wet	damp	moist	soggy
wonderful	magnificent	marvelous	splendid
wrong	improper	incorrect	false

Beginning a Writing Workshop

Introduction

A writing workshop began for the students in your class the first time you read a story to them and wrote on the chalkboard with them. This was when you began to develop background knowledge for each one of your students. Everything you do and say while reading a story and writing with your students relates to what they will do when they write for themselves.

Students will write their own stories in much the same manner as any published author. With guidance from you, they will think of an idea, write a first draft, confer with peers, revise their work, edit, confer with a teacher, and finally publish their work. This process is common to most student writers.

The purpose of the lessons in the following pages is to guide you through the process of preparing your students for their own writing workshop. As with most things, beginning is the hardest part. The first few lessons take some time, but they build the children's interest in writing their stories, and they give them ideas on which to rely in the future. This will allow you to work individually with more children during each writing workshop session. Your enthusiasm about your writing workshop during these lessons will set the tone for the remaining writing workshop sessions. Writing workshop can and should become the children's "best thing about school" because it is a truly creative time for each child. It is an opportunity for both the analytical and the global learner (right-brained and left-brained child) to excel.

Elements of a Story

Story Elements

Activity:

Students will identify the major elements of a story: setting, characters, problem, and solution.

Materials:

- *Aunt Isabel Tells a Good One* by Kate Duke (Puffin Books, 1994)
- chart paper
- marking pen

Preparation:

No preparation is required.

Directions:

In the book *Aunt Isabel Tells a Good One*, Penelope asks her Aunt Isabel to tell her a story. Together they develop a list of elements that a story needs if it is to be interesting and exciting.

The elements of a story are the setting (where and when the story takes place), the characters, the problem, and the solution.

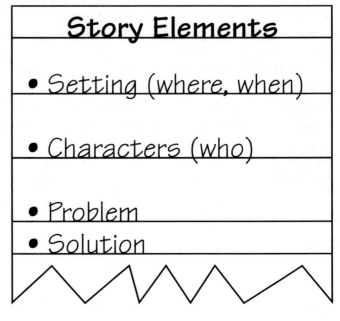

Read the title of the book to the students, pointing out the location of the capital and lowercase letters. Also read the author's name, pointing out that the author of this book is also the illustrator.

Now, read the story together, following this format:

Page 1: After reading page 1, stop and ask the children what two things Aunt Isabel says a good story needs (where and when: the setting). Write these responses on the chart paper. Continue reading the story.

Page 5: After reading page 5, ask the children what else Aunt Isabel says a story needs (who: the characters). Add this to the chart paper. Continue reading the story.

Page 9: After reading page 9, ask what else the book says that a story needs (the problem). Add this to the chart paper. Continue reading the story.

Page 23: After reading page 23, ask the children to tell what happens in this part of the story. Ask the students if there is still a problem, and when they answer no, ask why not. Add the word "solution" to the chart paper. Finish reading the story.

(**Note:** The pages in the book are not numbered. You will need to count.)

Title the chart you have made with the words "Story Elements." Review with the children the fact that good stories have these elements: a setting, characters, a problem, and a solution. Post your chart in the classroom for the children's future reference.

Parts of a Story

Story Parts

Activity:

Students will identify the three primary parts of a story and connect them with the basic story elements.

Materials:

- any favorite storybook
- chart paper
- marking pen

Preparation:

1. Select any favorite story and preread it for the story elements: setting, characters, problem, and solution.

2. Prepare the frame for a large story web on chart paper. A story web lists all the elements of a story.

Directions:

Let the students know that there are three parts to every good story: the beginning, the middle, and the ending. In many stories, the story elements appear in particular parts. The beginning usually contains the setting and the introduction of the characters. Some additional character development may occur and the problem appears in the middle of the story. The problem is solved and the story concluded in the ending section of the story. Stories written according to this structure are the simplest to write. (Do not be surprised if many stories your students write in the future are three pages in length when published: one page for each part of the story.)

Read to the students the story you have selected. When finished, complete the story web as a class. After completing the web, ask the children in which part of the story each element is introduced. Add this information to your web. Title the chart "Parts of a Story."

Display the chart in the classroom for the children's future reference.

Parts of a Story
• Beginning
–Setting
–Characters Introduced
• Middle
–Characters Developed
–Problem(s)
• Ending
–Solution(s)

Story Idea Charts

Subjects

Activity:

Students will identify possible story subjects.

Materials:

- any favorite storybook
- chart paper or a large piece of construction paper
- marking pens

Preparation:

Select a favorite story and preread it for plot.

Directions:

The idea charts on this page through page 86 are intended to encourage the children's interest and enthusiasm in writing their own stories. They will also help authors who are experiencing writer's block. The lists created through these activities are not meant to be all-inclusive. Rather, they are meant to encourage the children's own ideas. A one-page list is adequate.

The paper on which the charts are created may be cut into or mounted on a particular theme shape. The shape should contain several component pieces such as an ice-cream cone, train, rainbow, or traffic sign.

Each idea chart should be done as a separate lesson, and it is recommended that they be completed on consecutive days before the children begin writing their own stories.

To do a subject chart, first read your preselected story. Afterwards, ask the students to tell you its subject— what it is about. Then ask them to name the basic subjects of other stories they know and enjoy. Begin writing their ideas on chart or construction paper. Then ask them to brainstorm for other things a story might be about. If and when they get stuck, share a personal experience such as, "I could write a story about going to the zoo because I have been to the zoo." This will encourage them to think about things they have done, as well.

While the children are thinking of ideas, title the chart paper "What Can Stories Be About?"

After the lesson, display the list for the children's reference.

What Can Stories Be About?
1. soccer game
2. vacation
3. visiting Grandma
4. birthday party
5. pet
6. school
7. going to a friend's house

Characters

Activity:

Students will identify possible story characters.

Materials:

- any favorite storybook
- chart paper or a large piece of construction paper
- marking pens

Preparation:

Select a favorite story and preread it for easily identifiable characters.

Directions:

Read the selected story aloud. Afterwards, ask the students to identify the story's characters. Then ask them to name characters in other stories they know.

As they are thinking, title a sheet of chart paper "Who or What Can Stories Be About?" pointing out the generic nature of each of the characters they are naming. (For example, Stuart Little is a mouse, and Flat Stanley is a boy.)

Now ask the students to brainstorm for "Who or What Can Stories Be About?" Write their ideas on your chart paper. If they have difficulty, suggest character types in some of your favorite stories. Encourage them to do the same.

When complete, display the list for the children's reference.

Who or What Can Stories Be About?

1. princess

2. ghost

3. teacher

4. birthday party

5. dog

6. children

7. parents

Story Idea Charts

Setting

Activity:

Students will identify possible story settings.

Materials:

- any favorite storybook
- chart paper or a large piece of construction paper
- marking pens

Preparation:

Select a favorite story and preread it for setting (where and when).

Directions:

To do a setting chart, first read your preselected story. Afterwards, ask the students to tell you its setting, where and when it takes place. Then ask them to name the basic settings of other stories they know and enjoy. Begin writing their ideas on chart paper. Then ask them to brainstorm for other settings a story might include. If and when they have difficulty, share a personal experience such as, "I went to the shopping mall yesterday. I could write a story that takes place in a mall." This will encourage the students to think about places they have been, as well.

While the children are thinking of ideas, title the chart "Where Can Stories Take Place?"

After the lesson, display the list for the children's reference.

Where Can Stories Take Place?

1. store

2. school

3. home

4. castle

5. cave

6. museum

7. fire station

Story Idea Charts

Problem

Activity:

Students will identify possible story problems.

Materials:

- any favorite storybook
- chart paper or a large piece of construction paper
- marking pens

Preparation:

1. Select a favorite story and preread it for the central problem.
2. Brainstorm for problems you have personally experienced and make a list. Also make a list of problems you have never experienced.

Directions:

To complete a problem chart, first read your preselected story. Afterwards, ask the students to tell you its central problem. Then ask them to name the basic problems in other stories they know. Discuss some of these ideas.

Share a personal experience problem with the students, such as "I could write a story about having a flat tire because my car had a flat tire the other day on the way home from school."

Also share a few ideas you could not easily write, for example, "It would be difficult to write a believable story about being lost in the jungle because I have never been lost in a jungle." Use your preparatory lists to help you with these ideas.

Encourage the students to think about problems they have had or problems that have happened to their family. While the children are thinking of ideas, title the chart paper "What Kinds of Problems Can Be Found in Stories?" Add their ideas to the chart.

Afterwards, display the list for the children's reference.

What Kinds of Problems Can Be Found in Stories?

1. getting lost

2. losing something

3. being scared

4. getting hurt

5. getting angry

6. being wrongly accused

Story Idea Charts

Beginnings

Activity:

Students will identify possible beginnings for stories.

Materials:

- several favorite storybooks
- chart paper or a large piece of construction paper
- marking pens

Preparation:

Select several favorite stories and preread them for good beginning sentences.

Directions:

To make a beginnings chart, first read the beginnings of your preselected stories. Afterwards, ask the students to tell you their beginning sentences. Reread them, if necessary. If desired, have the students look at other storybooks in your classroom for additional beginnings.

Ask the students to brainstorm answers to the question, "How can stories start?" Explain that the beginning words of some stories tell what kind of stories they will be. For example, "Once upon a time" indicates it will be a fairy tale. If the story is not a fairy tale, it will probably begin with different words.

While the children are thinking of ideas, title the chart paper "How Can Stories Begin?" Make a list of the children's ideas. Be sure to give them time to think since the best ideas often come after awhile.

Should the children have difficulty thinking of ideas, encourage them with some of your own. Afterwards, display the completed list for the children's reference.

Note: This activity can be done now or after the children have been writing stories for awhile if you notice that most of their stories begin with the same words.

How Can Stories Begin?

1. Have you ever wondered about . . .

2. Once upon a time . . .

3. A long time ago . . .

4. When I was little . . .

5. Yesterday . . .

6. When my grandma was a little girl . . .

Teacher Writes a Story

Activity:

The purpose of this lesson is to demonstrate for the students how to write a story.

Materials:

- any favorite story
- chart paper
- marking pens
- chalkboard or overhead projector

Preparation:

1. Select a favorite story and preread it for all the story elements.

2. Think of an idea about which you can write a story. Be sure that you know the elements of your story. It is difficult to think while you are writing in front of the children.

Directions:

During this lesson the process of writing a story will be modeled. The process of publishing will be modeled in a later lesson. This lesson should take approximately twenty minutes to complete.

To begin, read your preselected story. Ask the children to name the various elements within the story. Write these on chart paper.

Tell the children that today during the writing workshop you will show them how to write a story. Explain that they have a job to do while you are writing your story: it will be their job to use their eyes, their ears, and their brains. They are to use their eyes to watch everything that you do. They are to use their ears to listen to everything that you say. They are to use their brains to remember what they see and hear so they will know how to write a story.

Who? Where?

What? When?

Problem? Solution?

Modeling Writing

Teacher Writes a Story *(cont.)*

Before you begin writing, model thinking about your story. Think aloud:

"What are some things that I know about that I could write a story about?

I could write a story about . . .

I think I'll write a story about . . .

Where will my story take place?

Who will be in my story?

What will the problem be?

How will I solve the problem?

What words will start my story?"

Now, write your story for the children, using the chalkboard or overhead projector. Make some or all of the following mistakes while writing the story:

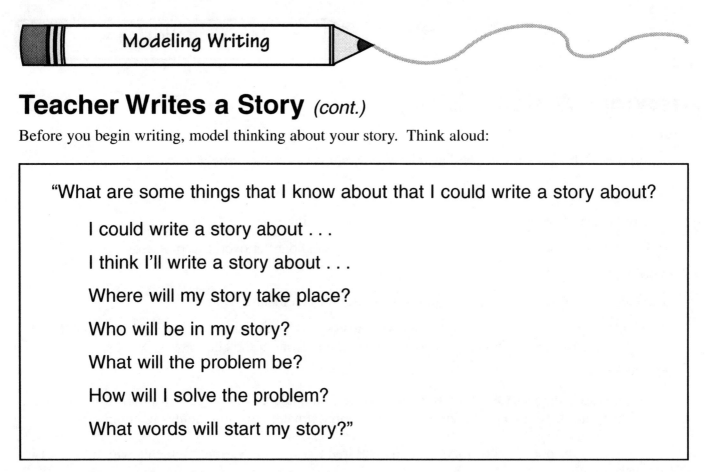

- omit some words — The went to the park.

- omit some capital letters — I saw mr. Jones.

- omit some punctuation marks — We saw fish lizards and monkeys.

- use some incorrect words — I lide there shoes.

- use some incorrect spellings — She wint to the movies.

Reread your story often while writing. Add any missing words. Correct incorrect words by drawing one line through them and writing the correct word above them. Correct spelling and punctuation errors.

After you have finished, have the children tell everything they saw and heard you do while you were writing your story. Record their responses on chart paper. Post the chart for future reference. Also have the students tell you your story elements. Add them to your chart paper.

Establishing the Rules for the Writing Workshop

Activity:

This lesson is designed to establish the rules for the writing workshop. The chart created will also guide the children as they work.

Materials:

- chart paper or a large piece of construction paper
- markers (a variety of colors)

Preparation:

Decide on the rules and guidelines you want the children to adhere to during your writing workshop time.

Directions:

This is a brief lesson done on the day the children begin writing their first story. The information given to the children should go something like this:

Now that we are ready to begin writing a story, you need to know what is expected of you during the writing workshop. Just as you have rules at home and we have rules at school, there are rules for the writing workshop.

These are the things that you are expected to do during the writing workshop. (Write each item on paper, using a different color for each item.)

1. Put the date at the top of each page.
2. Write the page number inside a circle at the top of each page.
3. Instead of erasing, draw one line through a mistake.
4. Save everything.
5. Do your best work.

Title the chart "Writing Workshop Rules" and hang it so the children can see it. Refer to it often so the children learn the rules.

After you have reviewed the rules, the students are ready to begin writing their first story.

Note: The management of materials is easier if the children use a spiral-bound notebook for their drafts. This notebook and the finished copies for publication can be kept in a pocket folder.

If the children will not be using a spiral notebook, staple several sheets of writing paper together.

The Writing Process

How to Publish a Story

Activity:

This lesson is designed to establish the steps of the writing process. The chart created will also guide the children during your writing workshop.

Materials:

- chart paper or a large piece of construction paper
- markers (a variety of colors)

Preparation:

Decide on the steps your students will take to publish their stories.

Directions:

Explain to the students that now that they have learned how to write a story, they will need to learn how to publish that story into a book. Tell them the following steps (or your own version), writing the steps on chart paper as you state them. (Use a different color for each step.)

How to Publish a Story

1. Think of an idea.

2. Write your story.

3. Read your story, pointing to each word as you read it. (Add any missing words, capital letters, and periods.)

4. Read your story to a partner, pointing to each word.

5. Revise your story, adding more details to make your story better.

6. Edit your story, checking for capital letters and periods.

7. Sign up for a writing conference.

8. Illustrate your story, making a title page and a cover.

9. When your story is ready to be bound, place it on the tray.

Title your completed chart "How to Publish a Story" and hang the chart so the children can see it. Refer to it often so the children learn to use it themselves.

This lesson should be done the second day of your writing workshop. Should any of your students tell you they have finished their story before this lesson is taught, have them put their story away and tell them that during the next writing workshop session you will give them further instructions. Ask them to read a book during the remaining writing workshop time.

The Writing Process

The Peer Conference

Activity:

Students will learn to conduct a peer conference.

Materials:

- previously modeled story (pages 87 and 88)
- marking pen

Preparation:

Complete the activities on pages 87 and 88.

Directions:

A peer conference is the first opportunity for an author to receive feedback about his or her story. Both children have a job to do during a peer conference. The author is the reader who brings his or her writing notebook to the conference. The peer is the listener who brings ideas to the conference.

When the children have completed a draft of their story, they are ready for a peer conference. Establish the following guidelines for a peer conference:

1. The author and peer sit close together with their knees touching. (This helps keep the noise level to a minimum and helps to keep them engaged in their jobs.)
2. The author brings his or her writing notebook and reads the story. The peer is the listener and thinker. He or she listens carefully to the story and then gives one or two ideas as to how the author can make the story better.
3. Peer listeners must give ideas for revising (making the story better).
4. After reading the story, the author and peer discuss ideas that will improve the story.
5. The author thanks the peer and returns to his or her writing to revise the story.

Give the children several examples of ideas a peer listener might give an author. For example:

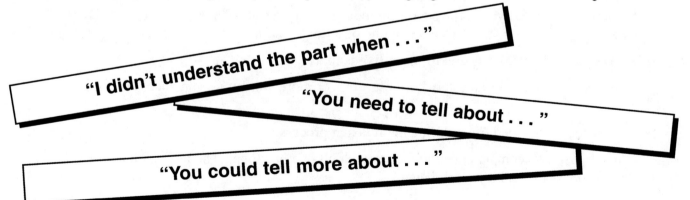

"I didn't understand the part when . . ."

"You need to tell about . . ."

"You could tell more about . . ."

Before the students conduct a peer conference on their own, model one for them, using the story you wrote previously or another you have written. It is helpful to have a peer (another teacher) do the modeling with you, if possible.

The Writing Process

Revising

Activity:

Students will learn to revise their writing.

Materials:

- story on chart paper
- marking pen

Preparation:

Rewrite your story from the previous activity (pages 87 and 88) onto chart paper.

Directions:

Revising for primary grade children is usually the process of adding more to a story to make it better. This is difficult because most of the children will think their story is complete (and perfect) when they have decided they are finished.

This lesson is built upon two previous lessons, Teacher Writes a Story (pages 87 and 88) and The Peer Conference (page 91). Using the same story you used for The Peer Conference lesson, revise your story. Remind the children of their "job" when you are working on a story. They are to use their eyes and ears and minds. This is your story, and they are not helping you to write it, but they must follow everything you do and be able later to tell you the steps.

While working, you can think aloud along these lines:

"Today I am going to work on my story to make it better. This is called revising. Let me think; when I had a conference with my partner, he gave me some good ideas for making my story better."

Follow these steps when modeling the revision process:

- Review all the ideas you received during the peer conference. Think of some more ideas of your own to improve your story. Decide on one or more of the ideas to incorporate into your story.

- Demonstrate the use of a caret to insert words in a sentence.

- Demonstrate the use of an asterisk to insert one or more words or a sentence into the appropriate place in the story.

- Reread the story aloud often during the revising process.

- When revising is complete, reread the story aloud one last time. Then say aloud, "Now I have revised my story, and it is even better."

Tell the children that you expect to see both the caret and the asterisk used in their stories. In fact, that is how you will know they have revised their stories.

The Writing Process

Editing

Activity:

Students will learn to edit their writing.

Materials:

- story on chart paper or an overhead transparency
- red marker
- red pens
- conference sign-up sheet (page 94)

Preparation:

Write a simple story or use the story from Teacher Writes a Story (pages 87 and 88). Copy the story onto chart paper or an overhead transparency, omitting some capitals and punctuation.

Directions:

This lesson is built upon two previous lessons, Teacher Writes a Story (pages 87 and 88) and The Peer Conference (page 91). In order to complete this lesson, understand that editing for primary grade children is the process of checking for capital letters at the beginning of each sentence, punctuation marks at the end of sentences, and the correct spelling of frequently used words (or teacher-specified words).

Model for the students the process of editing. Remind the children that their job when you are writing is to use their eyes and ears only. This is your story, and they are not writing it, but they must pay careful attention to what you do so that they can do the same when it is their turn. Think aloud, "Now that I have revised my story to make it better, I am almost ready to sign up for a conference with my teacher. But first I have to edit my story. What does that mean? I remember; editing means looking for mistakes in my writing like missing capital letters, no periods, and wrong spellings."

Use a red marker as you model editing the story. As you read your story aloud, listening for the pauses at the ends of sentences, give "hints" so the children know when to put in a punctuation mark. For example, "I stopped reading after (blank), so I must need a period (exclamation point, question mark) after that word. Let's see, does that sentence make sense?" (Reread the sentence and have the children give the silent signal, thumbs-up, to indicate yes or thumbs-down to indicate no.)

It may prove helpful to edit for punctuation marks in the entire story first. Then reread the story and edit for capital letters following each end punctuation mark. Then think aloud, "Now, I am finished editing my story, and I can sign up for a conference with my teacher."

Show the students the conference sign-up sheet and tell them where it is kept and how to use it.

Be sure to provide several red pens that the children can use for editing their own work. Tell them where the red pens will be kept. (The use of the red pens is very motivational for the children, and they allow you to quickly scan their stories to see the editing they have done prior to your conference.)

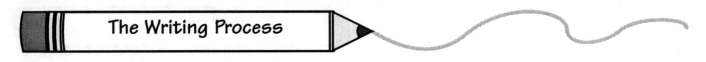

The Writing Process

Conference Sign-Ups

Sign up for a conference with the teacher after you have edited your writing.

Time	Name

The Writing Process

Spelling: Give It a Go

Activity:

Students will learn a procedure for checking their spelling.

Materials:

- Spelling: Give It a Go sheet (1 per student plus extras)
- marking pen
- chart paper
- children's dictionaries

Preparation:

Make a large version of the Spelling: Give It a Go sheet on chart paper.

Directions:

Children move through the developmental stages of spelling at their own pace. Many children resist writing at school because they do not know how to spell the words they want to write. Discuss with the children the fact that they are not expected to know how to spell every word they will use in their stories. Dictionaries are there to help them. Show them several dictionaries and explain how to use them.

Show the large version of Spelling: Give It a Go on the chart paper. Explain that this sheet is for words that are very important to their story but that they are unsure how to spell. If they do not think they spelled it correctly in their story, they should circle it and then write it on side A of their own sheets. Then, as you circulate during your writing workshop time, you will stop and help them look in the dictionaries for the correct spelling (or they may look themselves). They can then write the correct spelling on side B of their sheets. You will check to be sure it is correct. Then they can copy the correct words into their stories.

Model the use of the sheet on the chart paper. Let the students use the dictionaries to find the correct spellings.

If you feel your students are not yet ready for dictionaries, simply have them list the words they are unsure of, and then you can write their correct spellings as you circulate during writing workshop time.

Spelling: Give It a Go	
A	**B**
thay	they
scool	school
teechr	teacher
hapy	

The Writing Process

Spelling: Give It a Go *(cont.)*

Write the word you are not sure about on side A. Use the dictionary. Write the correct spelling on side B.

A	B

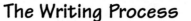

The Writing Process

Writing Titles

Activity:

Students will learn the guidelines behind writing story titles.

Materials:

- several books with correctly written titles
- marking pen
- rulers
- chart paper
- lined and unlined paper
- pencils

Preparation:

No preparation is required.

Directions:

Let the students know that when writing a title, the first and last words begin with a capital letter and any other important words in the title are also capitalized. Insignificant words such as *the, and, an,* and *a* are not capitalized.

Hold up the books one at a time. Read each title with the children. Point out the location of the capital letters in each title. After several examples, ask the children if they noticed anything the same about the location of capital letters in the titles. Record their answers on the chart paper. Continue until the children figure out that the first and last words in the title always start with a capital letter and that other words (except little words such as *the, and, an,* and *a*) are capitalized, also. Give the students hints if they need them.

Demonstrate writing a title correctly. First, use lined paper and write a title on it. Then use unlined paper, and show them how to draw a rule line so that their titles are straight. Allow the students an opportunity to write a title on both kinds of paper.

At the end of the lesson, post the guidelines for writing titles (on the chart paper) so that the students can refer to them, as needed.

Little Red Riding Hood

Goldilocks and the Three Bears

Peter Rabbit

Writing Workshop Mini-Lessons

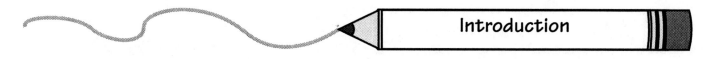

Introduction

Positive words of encouragement and an enthusiastic attitude are paramount for developing authors in the primary grades. Primary grade children have a natural interest in writing, and every one of them can be successful if they believe they can. Celebrate each child's accomplishments!

Primary grade children usually begin by writing personal narrative stories for which they will draw on their own personal experiences. As they become more adventurous with their writing, they may develop stories similar to those they have heard or read in class. They may even incorporate some of the things they have learned in other curricular areas. Some of the children will model their first story after the one you wrote during the modeling lesson. Do not be surprised or disappointed since they feel this a "safe" subject choice.

Should you feel the need to move a child on to another subject area because several stories have been quite similar, discuss individually with the child some other ideas and help him or her to select one. Then discuss the elements of a story with the child before writing begins. This will help the child feel confident about writing the story.

All stories a child works on do not need to be published. Sometimes a child may decide that he does not like the story. The child should be encouraged to move on to a new story. Perhaps the child may want to return to that story at a later time or perhaps not. Either decision is appropriate.

All pieces chosen for publication should look professional when complete. Every published book should have a cover, a title page, and binding.

You will find that the writing abilities of the children in your class will vary greatly, even more so than in their reading abilities. Joyfully accept what children write since your encouragement will help them to explore and to grow. With support and celebration, each child will be able to develop his or her writing skills to their fullest.

| | Parts of Speech: Nouns | |

People, Places, and Things

Activity:

Students will identify nouns and categorize them into people, places, and things.

(**Note:** If you completed the activities on pages 32–49, the activities on pages 100–102 will reinforce or extend those lessons. If you have not used any of the previous lessons, you may wish to review them to determine if any are necessary for your class before completing the following activities.)

Materials:

- chart paper or a large piece of construction paper
- markers
- *A Cache of Jewels and Other Collective Nouns* by Ruth Heller

Preparation:

Label three pieces of chart paper or construction paper, each with one of the following: Person, Place, Thing.

Directions:

Remind the students that a noun is a word that names a person, place, or thing. (If appropriate, add "idea" to this list. Introduce examples such as happiness, freedom, and love. Adapt the noun lessons to include an idea column.) Together, read *A Cache of Jewels and Other Collective Nouns* by Ruth Heller. Discuss the nouns in the book.

Next, divide the students into three cooperative groups. Give each group one of the prepared pieces of chart paper. Each group is to provide a list of words that fit into its given category.

When the lists are complete, ask each group to share its list with the other groups. Additional words may be added by the whole group, if space allows.

Note: The goal is for the list to be generic. For example, building is a good common noun for the list, but the proper noun Sears Tower is not. Likewise, dog and teacher are good ideas, but Sparky and Mrs. Jones are not.

Following are some sample lists. Use the words to help the students, as needed.

Person	Place	Thing
teacher	house	fish
doctor	cave	dog
pilot	school	desk
nurse	store	pencil
mother	hospital	pizza
dentist	mansion	flower

Parts of Speech: Nouns

Noun-mania

Activity:

Students will list as many nouns as they can in five minutes.

Materials:

- tagboard
- noun sheet (page 102; 1 per student)
- laminating machine (optional)
- permanent markers
- pencils
- scissors (one per student)

Preparation:

1. Enlarge the noun pattern letters on page 102 and copy them onto tagboard. (Make the letters as large as possible, one per tagboard, if you can).

2. Laminate the letters, if desired.

Directions:

Remind children that nouns are words that name people, places, or things.

Pass out the noun sheet to each child. Have students cut out the letters and arrange them to spell NOUN. Then ask students to write as many nouns on the letters N, O, U, and N as they can in five minutes. At the end of five minutes, have the children share the words they wrote. Record their ideas on the large tagboard letters. Display the letters for the students' future reference.

Note: If desired, tell the students ahead of time that this is a PIG activity. (It can be done with a Partner, Individually, or in a Group.)

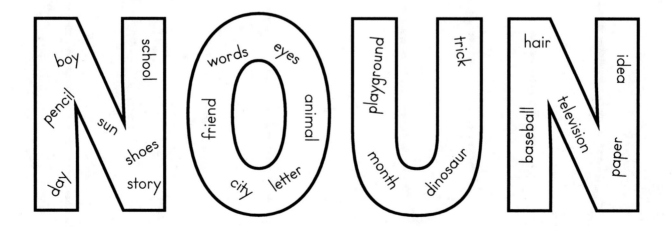

Parts of Speech: Nouns

Noun-mania *(cont.)*

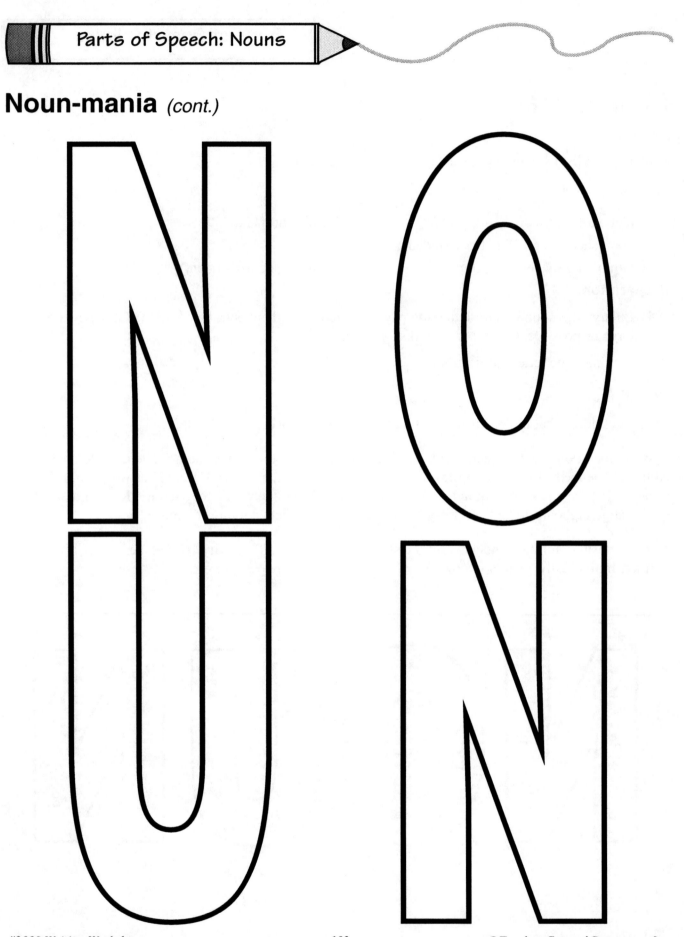

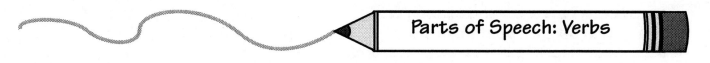

Parts of Speech: Verbs

Verb-mania

Activity:

Students will list as many verbs as they can in five minutes.

(**Note:** If you completed the activities on pages 50–64, the activities on pages 103–107 will reinforce or extend those lessons. If you have not used any of the previous lessons, you may wish to review them to determine if any are necessary for your class before completing the following activities.)

Materials:

- tagboard
- permanent markers
- verb sheet (page 104; 1 per student)
- pencils
- laminating machine (optional)
- scissors

Preparation:

1. Enlarge the verb pattern letters on page 104 and copy them onto tagboard. (Make the letters as large as possible, one per tagboard, if you can.)
2. Laminate the letters, if desired.

Directions:

Remind children that verbs are usually words that show action. They are words that tell what people, places, or things do.

Pass out the verb sheet to each child. Have students cut out the letters and arrange them to spell VERB. Then ask students to write as many verbs on the letters VERB as they can in five minutes. At the end of five minutes, have the children share the words they wrote. Record their ideas on the large tagboard letters. Display the letters for the students' future reference.

Note: If desired, tell the students ahead of time that this is a PIG activity. (It can be done with a Partner, Individually, or in a Group.)

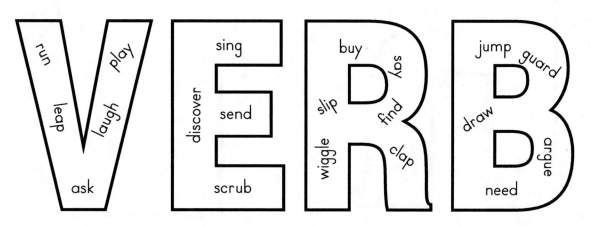

Parts of Speech: Verbs

Verb-mania *(cont.)*

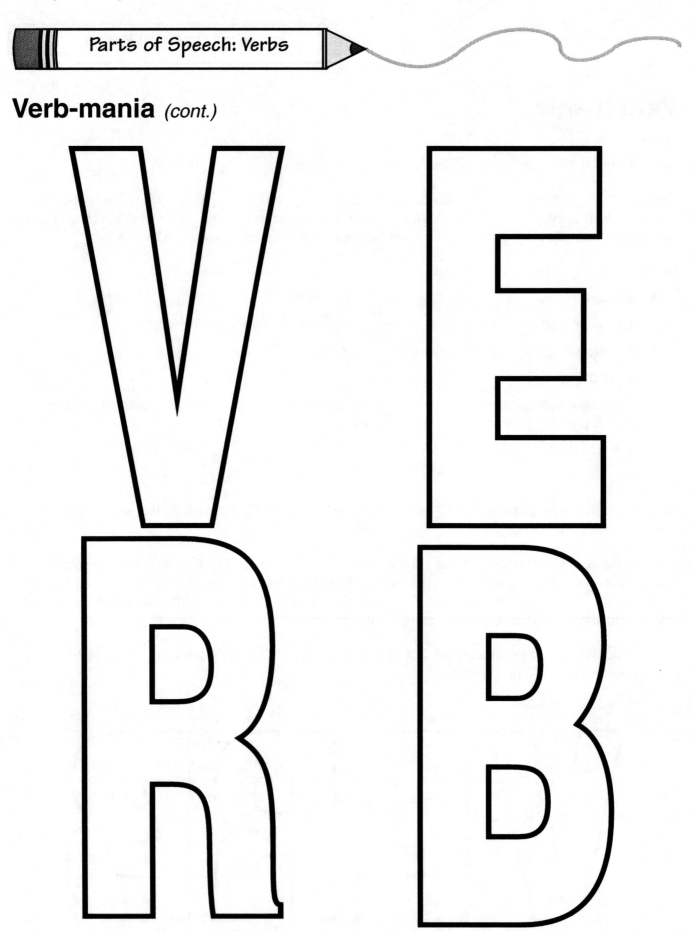

Parts of Speech: Verbs

Verb Tenses

Activity:

Students will learn about verb tenses.

Materials:

- *I Think, I Thought and Other Tricky Verbs* by Marvin Terban
- pocket chart(s)

- index cards
- sentence strips
- marking pen

Preparation:

1. Write action verbs on index cards, at least one per student. Make one half of the cards present-tense verbs and the other half past tense.

2. Using the sentence strips, write one sentence for each verb card, leaving a blank line (the size of an index card) for the verb.

3. Display as many sentences as possible in a pocket chart.

Directions:

Read aloud *I Think, I Thought and Other Tricky Verbs.* Then discuss verb tenses with the children. Note for the students that the past tense of most verbs is formed by adding *d* or *ed* to the present tense. However, short-vowel words require a double consonant before adding *ed*, and some words change completely.

Pass out the verb cards to the students. Instruct the students to silently read the sentences in the pocket chart. Each child who finds a sentence that his or her verb fits can slip the card into the blank space of the sentence.

When all the sentences have been completed, change the sentences and continue as before. You may wish to return the cards to the students who have used theirs, shuffling them so that they are working with different verbs. This will keep all students focused on the activity.

Once sentences have been completed, have the class read them aloud in unison. To extend the activity, have students or groups come up with alternate verbs for each sentence.

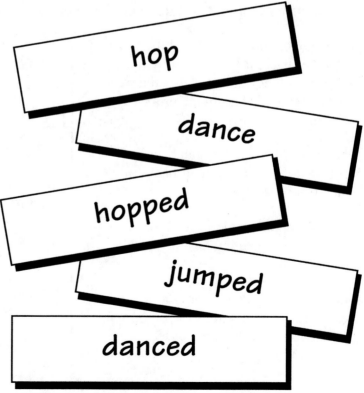

Parts of Speech: Verbs

Verb Tense Game

Activity:

Students will identify verbs and sort them according to tense.

Materials:

- index cards (at least 1 per student)
- chart paper or a large piece of construction paper
- marking pen
- tape

Preparation:

1. Write a verb on each index card. Use present and past tenses of verbs.
2. Prepare a graph on the chart paper with two columns. Label the columns Present Tense and Past Tense.

Directions:

In this game, each student will identify a verb placed on his or her back and attach it to the graph in its appropriate column.

Tape one verb card to the back of each player. Have the students choose partners. Each student will then ask questions of his or her partner to identify the verb attached to his or her back. The partner may answer yes or no to the questions. The partner may also pantomime the verb.

When the child has identified the word on his or her back, it is removed by the teacher, and the student places the word on the prepared chart in the proper column.

Play ends when all children have identified the verbs on their backs or when time has expired.

When complete, review the graph with the students, changing any incorrectly placed cards.

Note: As the students learn more about verb tenses, add columns to your graph, particularly for the future tense.

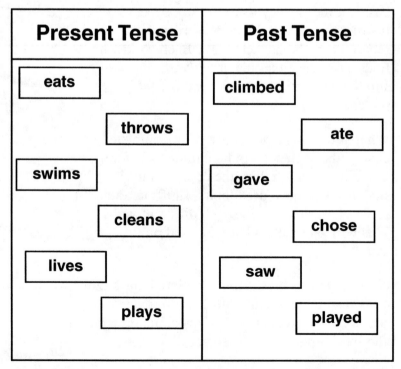

Present Tense	Past Tense
eats	climbed
throws	ate
swims	gave
cleans	chose
lives	saw
plays	played

Parts of Speech: Verbs

Verbs Go Round

Activity:

Students will name present-tense verbs and match them to their past-tense partners.

Materials:

- none

Preparation:

There is no preparation required.

Directions:

Choose one child. Ask that child to think of a present-tense verb. He or she should whisper the verb to you for confirmation of its tense.

The class forms a large circle with the chosen child in the middle. As the circle slowly moves around, the child inside the circle names the verb and tags one of the students in the outer circle. The student who was tagged must then say the past tense of the verb. If the past-tense verb is correct, the two children trade places. If the past-tense verb is incorrect, the child inside the circle tags someone else. (Be sure that the new child in the middle confirms his or her chosen word with you, as well. Do this until you are confident that they know their present-tense verbs. Alternately, have the students draw present-tense verbs from a bag that you have prepared ahead of time.) Continue play until everyone has had a turn to be inside the circle.

Parts of Speech: Pronouns

The Nouns Are Missing!

Activity:

Students will replace nouns with pronouns.

Materials:

- *Miss Nelson Is Missing!* by Harry Allard (Houghton Mifflin, 1985)
- chart paper
- marker
- chalkboard or overhead projector (optional)

Preparation:

Write on chart paper (or the chalkboard or an overhead projector transparency) several sentences containing nouns that can be replaced with pronouns.

Directions:

Let the students know that pronouns are words that take the place of nouns in a sentence. Provide them with several examples.

Read aloud the story *Miss Nelson Is Missing!* Discuss what a substitute teacher is and does, and discuss the meaning of the word substitute. Link this to the concept of pronouns substituting for nouns. Just for fun, ask each child to name a pronoun that could substitute for his or her own name.

Work with the children to read the sentences you prepared ahead of time, replacing the nouns with pronouns. On chart paper, make a list of the pronouns used in the sentences as well as any other pronouns the children know. Display the chart for the students' reference.

she   we   he   you

it   us   him

they

them   me   her

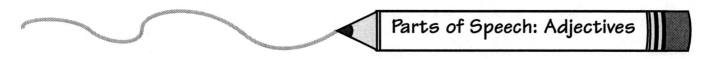

Parts of Speech: Adjectives

Describe It

Activity:

Students will learn to improve their writing through the addition of adjectives.

Materials:

- food item (suggestions: grapes, potato chips, apple slices, marshmallows, crackers, popcorn, gumdrops, jellybeans, or pretzels)
- chart paper

- marking pen
- writing paper
- markers or crayons

Preparation:

Prepare a sheet of chart paper by writing the title "Adjectives" at the top. In three columns under the title, write the headings Looks, Feels, and Tastes.

Directions:

Let the students know that adjectives are words that describe or tell about nouns or pronouns. They add details about the nouns or pronouns, telling what kind, how much, or how they compare.

Pass out the food item, one per child, instructing the students not to touch it. Ask the students to brainstorm for words that describe how the item looks. Record these words on the chart.

Next, instruct the students to touch the item and to brainstorm for words that describe how it feels. Record these words on the chart.

Finally, instruct the students to eat the item and brainstorm for words that describe how it tastes. (**Note:** Check for food allergies and make adjustments as needed.) Record these words on the chart.

When all describing words have been recorded, choral read the words. Then ask the students to each write three to five descriptive sentences about the food item, using some of the words on the chart. While the children are writing their sentences, allow them to enjoy more of the food item. When their sentences are complete, have the students use a crayon or marker to underline/circle the adjectives they used.

Display the class chart as a student reference for adjectives.

Parts of Speech: Adjectives

Bag It

Activity:

Students will describe an object with adjectives and use adjectives to guess one another's hidden object.

Materials:

- *Many Luscious Lollipops: A Book About Adjectives* by Ruth Heller
- chart paper
- marking pen
- paper lunch bags (1 per student and teacher)
- parent letter (page 111, 1 per student)
- stapler

Preparation:

1. Write each child's name on a bag.
2. Prepare a sample bag.
   - Write your name on the bag.
   - Select an item to put inside the bag.
   - Write five adjectives on the bag that describe the item.
   - Put the item in the bag and staple it closed.

Directions:

This activity can be done over two days. On the first day, read *Many Luscious Lollipops*. Together with the students, brainstorm for a list of adjectives and write them on chart paper. Display the chart for the students' reference.

Next, show the students your sample bag. Read the adjectives with them. Ask them to guess the object inside. Take as many guesses as they can offer. After a few minutes, open the bag and show them the object. Point out how each of the adjectives written on the bag describes the item.

Give each child his or her bag and a parent letter. Have them take the bags and letter home to complete for homework. They should each place an item (to be returned) in the bag and seal it closed, writing five adjectives on the bag. Let the students know that they must bring the bags back to school the next day.

On the second day, have the students share their bags. As they tell their adjectives, instruct the other students to listen. The child who is sharing can call on children with raised hands to make guesses about the object inside. After approximately five guesses, have the student open the bag to reveal its actual contents.

Add the students' adjectives to the class chart you began on the previous day. Continue to add adjectives to the chart, as desired. Encourage the children to use these and other adjectives when they are writing their stories.

Bag It: Parent Letter

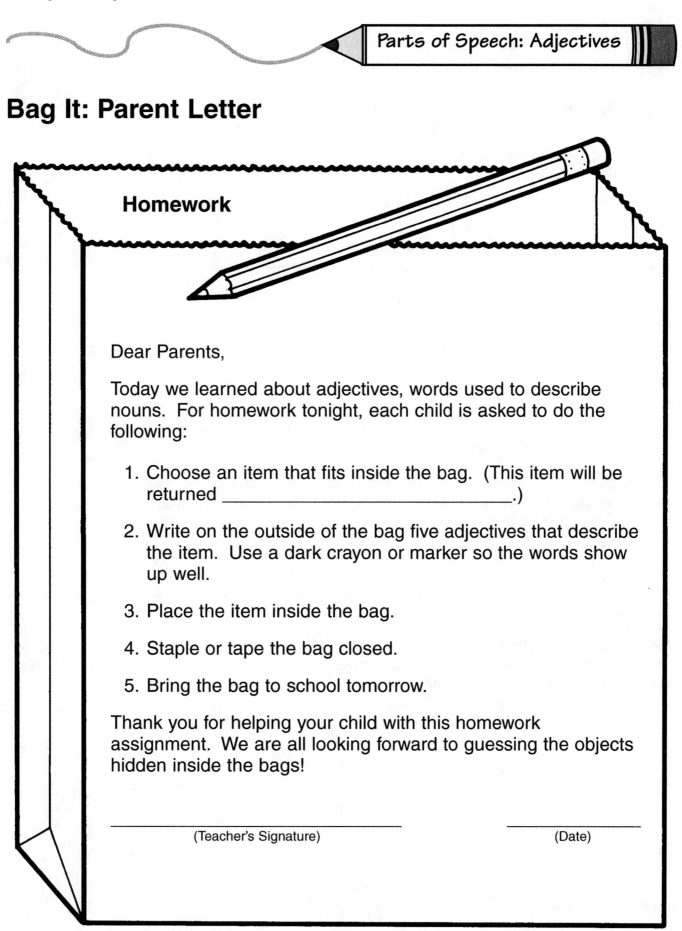

Homework

Dear Parents,

Today we learned about adjectives, words used to describe nouns. For homework tonight, each child is asked to do the following:

1. Choose an item that fits inside the bag. (This item will be returned _____.)

2. Write on the outside of the bag five adjectives that describe the item. Use a dark crayon or marker so the words show up well.

3. Place the item inside the bag.

4. Staple or tape the bag closed.

5. Bring the bag to school tomorrow.

Thank you for helping your child with this homework assignment. We are all looking forward to guessing the objects hidden inside the bags!

_____

(Teacher's Signature)

_____

(Date)

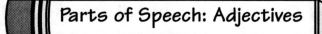

Parts of Speech: Adjectives

Animal Adjectives

Activity:

Students will write adjectives to describe an animal.

Materials:

- animal pictures (1 per student)
- white construction or drawing paper (1 per student)
- glue
- crayons or markers

- stapler, hole punch, and yarn or hole punch and binding rings
- poster board or colored construction paper (for book front and back)

Preparation:

Prepare a front and back cover for the class book. Use the poster board or colored construction paper. Title the book "Animal Adjectives."

Directions:

Distribute an animal picture and large white sheet of paper to each student. Have the students glue their animal pictures to the center of the white paper.

Instruct each student to brainstorm for adjectives to describe the animal in his or her picture. Each student can then write those adjectives around the picture, using crayons or markers to make the words bright and colorful. (Hint: If students use colors to match the animal, the colors can then serve as visual adjectives.)

When the pictures are complete, have each child read his or her page to the class. Collect all the pages and bind them into a book, adding the front and back covers. Keep the book on display for the students' perusal.

Note: This lesson can be done as a class by using a poster-size picture of an animal and having all the students work together to brainstorm for descriptive words. Glue the picture to a sheet of chart paper and record the adjectives in the borders, allowing each student to write one. Display the completed project for the students' reference.

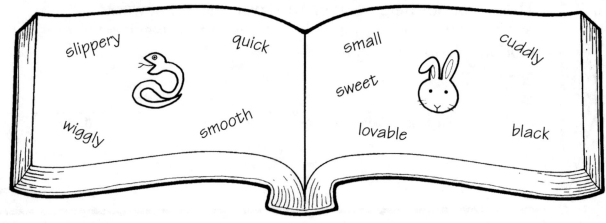

Colorful Writing

Activity:

Students will add adjectives to their writing to make it more interesting (colorful).

Materials:

- 1 first-draft story per student
- 1 crayon or marker per student

Preparation:

Each student will need to write a story.

Directions:

Tell the students that interesting writing is often described as being colorful. Explain that the word colorful means "full of interest."

Ask each child to review the story he or she has written, adding adjectives to make the writing more interesting (colorful). When they have done so, instruct them to review their writing once more, underlining (circling, highlighting) all the words that add color (interest) to their story.

When complete, have the students share their adjectives. List the adjectives (perhaps in a colorful rainbow pattern) on the chalkboard under the heading "Making Our Writing More Colorful."

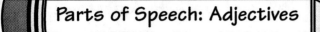

Parts of Speech: Adjectives

Colorful Words

Activity:

Students will determine if nouns and adjectives match, and if so, use them in a sentence.

Materials:

- Colorful Words Game Board (pages 115 and 116)
- colored pencils, markers, or crayons
- picture of pet, person, or toy (1 per player)
- glue
- die or spinner
- file folder
- marking pen
- index cards (1 per picture)
- scissors
- laminating machine (optional)

Preparation:

1. Color the game board and glue it to the file folder. If desired, glue the directions to the back.

2. Write an adjective in each square of the game board. Choose words that can describe a person, pet, or toy.

3. Cut the index cards in half. Mount the pictures on the card halves and fold them in half so they will stand. (These figures will be used as playing pieces.)

4. If desired, laminate the game board and playing pieces for durability.

Directions:

Two to four players can play this game. It is an excellent game for a learning center.

To play, each player chooses a playing piece. Choose a player to go first. Taking turns, the players roll or spin to determine how many squares to move. If the adjective the player lands on makes sense for his or her playing piece, the player uses the adjective and the playing piece object in a sentence. He or she remains on the square. If the word in the square does not make sense, the player must move back one square. Play then continues to that player's left.

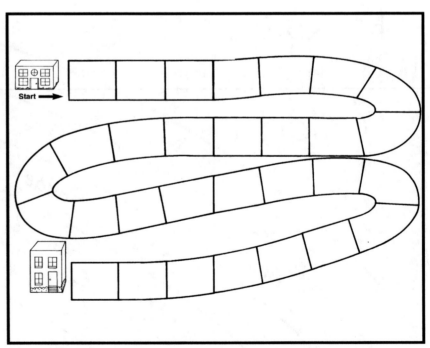

The first player to reach the finish square is the winner. Players do not need to roll or spin an exact number to land on finish.

Colorful Words Game Board

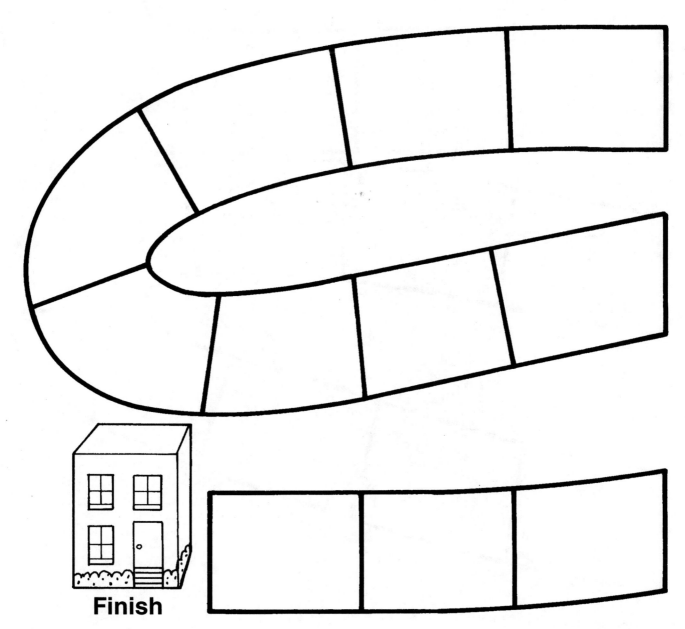

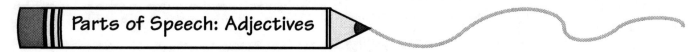

Parts of Speech: Adjectives

Colorful Words Game Board *(cont.)*

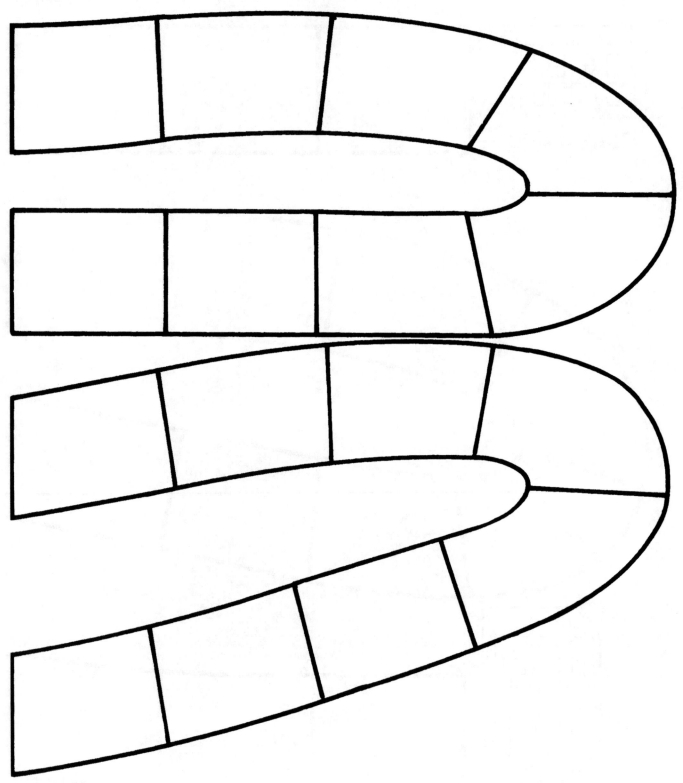

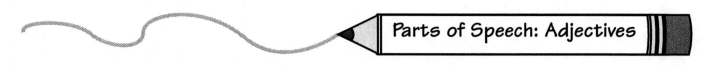

Parts of Speech: Adjectives

Multi-Adjectives

Activity:

Students will add a string of adjectives to an adjective-noun phrase.

Materials:

- index cards
- marking pen
- markers (1 per student)
- laminating machine (optional)

Preparation:

1. Write an adjective-noun phrase on several index cards, making at least one card for each student.
2. Laminate the cards, if desired.

Directions:

Students may work in small groups for this activity. Give each group several blank cards, enough so that each student in the group has one. Then give each group an adjective-noun phrase card.

Instruct each child in the group to add, one at a time, another adjective to the phrase. The child should say the phrase with the addition of his or her adjective before writing the adjective on his/her blank card. When the activity is complete, each group will have added one adjective per student to the initial phrase.

At the end of an allotted time, ask each group to share its multi-adjective phrase. Afterwards, exchange the phrase cards and distribute more blank cards so that the groups can try again.

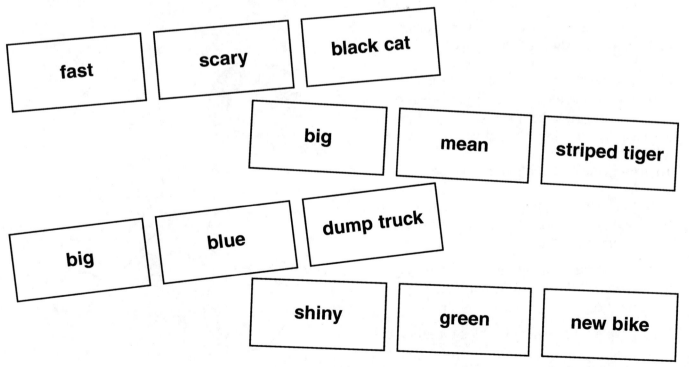

Parts of Speech: Adjectives

Bubbles, Bubbles, and More Bubbles!

Activity:

Students will write descriptions of an imaginary experience.

Materials:

- bottle of blowing bubbles
- bubble blowing wand (1 per student)
- outside area
- chart paper
- marking pen

- watercolor paints and paintbrushes
- drawing paper (1 sheet per student)
- thin, clear plastic (such as from dry-cleaner bags or plastic food wrap)

Preparation:

No preparation is required.

Directions:

As a prewriting activity, take the children outside with a container of bubbles and a blowing wand for each student. While the children blow bubbles, talk about the colors, shapes, sizes, and movement of their bubbles.

Back in the classroom, brainstorm what it might be like to float in a bubble. Begin the discussion by asking questions such as, "What would it feel like?" "Where would you go?" and "How long would your bubble ride last?" Encourage the children to use adjectives in their responses. Write their ideas on a sheet of chart paper.

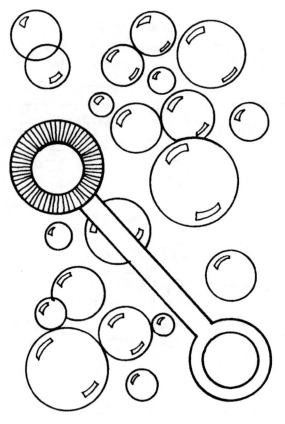

Instruct each student to write about his or her adventure inside a bubble, using the ideas on the chart to help. Ask them to use plenty of adjectives to make their writing come alive.

To display the children's work, do the following:

1. Let each child paint a sheet of drawing paper with watercolors. When it is dry, cut a large circle from it and glue the writing to it.

2. For a three-dimensional effect, loosely cover each child's project with a layer of thin, clear plastic.

3. Display the writing bubbles for all to read.

The Adjective Lady

Activity:

Students will list adjectives to describe an outlandish costume.

Materials:

- assortment of unusual and mismatched clothing (hat, sunglasses, bathrobe, jewelry, etc.)
- chart paper
- marking pen

Preparation:

1. Collect an unusual assortment of wearable items.
2. Arrange for a colleague to be in your class while you put on your costume over your regular clothing.

Directions:

Enter the classroom with great fanfare, and take time to enjoy the students' reactions. Then introduce yourself as the Adjective Lady (Gentleman).

Invite the students to observe your outfit closely. Engage them in using multiple adjectives to describe the Adjective Lady's attire. Focus their attention on individual items by removing them one at a time and holding them up for view. Record on chart paper the words the students use to describe the outfit.

When all items have been removed and piled on the floor, act confused and puzzled about the pile as if you are unaware of the Adjective Lady's visit to your room. Rave about the fabulous list of adjectives that has suddenly appeared.

Parts of Speech: Adverbs

Using Adverbs

Activity:

Students will learn to improve their writing through the addition of adverbs.

Materials:

- *Up, Up, and Away: A Book About Adverbs* by Ruth Heller
- chart paper
- tagboard
- scissors
- large brass paper fastener
- red, blue, and black markers

Preparation:

1. Cut a large circle from the tagboard.

2. Attach the tagboard circle to the center of a sheet of chart paper, affixing it in the center with the brass fastener. If desired, also cut the chart paper in a circle shape, keeping it larger than the tagboard circle.

Directions:

Tell the students that adverbs are words that describe verbs. They tell how, when, where, why, how much, or how often an action happened. Often they end with the letters "ly."

To help explain, use the following example:

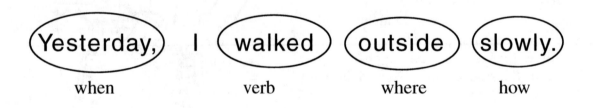

Have the students brainstorm a list of verbs. Record the verbs on the tagboard circle, writing them like spokes. Use the blue marker to write the verbs. When the circle is full, choral read the verbs.

Next, read *Up, Up, and Away: A Book About Adverbs*. Talk about the adverbs in the book. Then ask the students to brainstorm a list of adverbs that describe the verbs you have already written. Write these in red marker on the chart paper and also in spoke fashion. More than one adverb can be written for each verb, if desired. When the paper is full, choral read the adverbs on the paper.

Use the black marker to write a very large "I" in the center of the circle. "Write" a sentence by reading each set of words, beginning with I. Turn the center circle to match the verbs to other adverbs to see if they make sense.

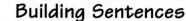

Building Sentences

Using Adverbs and Adjectives

Activity:

Students will locate adverbs and adjectives and use them in sentences.

Materials:

- task cards (page 122)
- glue
- scissors
- laminating machine (optional)
- writing paper
- magazines
- newspapers

Preparation:

Copy the task cards and laminate them for durability, if desired.

Directions:

Review adverbs and adjectives with the students. Let the students offer several examples of each.

Ask each child to select a task card. Using the supplied materials, have the children complete their chosen tasks. If you wish, have each child complete more than one task card.

Note: This activity can also be used to evaluate the children's understanding of the different parts of speech. Simply change the information on the task cards.

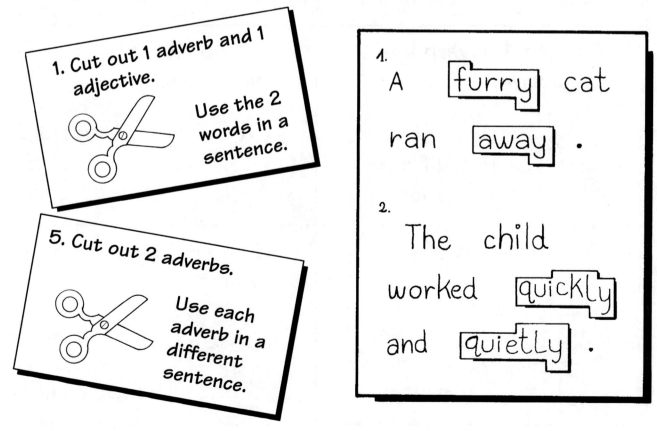

Building Sentences

Sentence Building Task Cards

1. Cut out 1 adverb and 1 adjective. 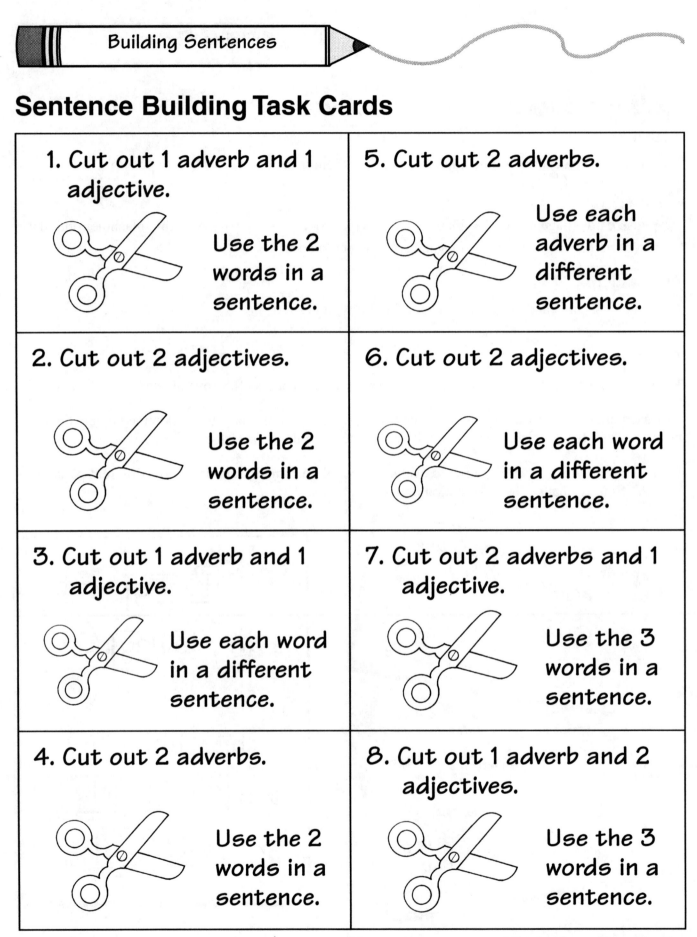 Use the 2 words in a sentence.	**5. Cut out 2 adverbs.** Use each adverb in a different sentence.
2. Cut out 2 adjectives. Use the 2 words in a sentence.	**6. Cut out 2 adjectives.** Use each word in a different sentence.
3. Cut out 1 adverb and 1 adjective. Use each word in a different sentence.	**7. Cut out 2 adverbs and 1 adjective.** Use the 3 words in a sentence.
4. Cut out 2 adverbs. Use the 2 words in a sentence.	**8. Cut out 1 adverb and 2 adjectives.** Use the 3 words in a sentence.

Possessing Possessives

Activity:

Students will say and write sentences that show possession.

Materials:

- chalkboard, overhead, or chart paper
- crayons, markers, or colored pencils
- drawing paper
- sentence strips

Preparation:

Prepare an example of each of the following activities to show the students.

Directions:

Explain the meaning of a possessive to the children, telling them that the possessive form of a noun denotes ownership. Give several oral examples.

On the board, overhead projector, or chart paper, show them how possessives are formed. Provide the following information:

- Forming the possessive of a singular noun is done by adding an apostrophe and an s.

    Examples: dentist's, girl's, cat's

- Forming the possessive of a plural noun ending in s is done by adding an apostrophe.

    Examples: brothers', Smiths', dogs'

- Forming the possessive of a plural noun that does not end in s is done by adding an apostrophe and an s.

    Examples: men's, children's, oxen's

The rest of this activity comes in two parts. First, ask each student to take something from his or her desk. Working with a partner, ask each child to tell the partner a sentence that shows his or her ownership of the item. Once done, have the partners exchange their items and offer a sentence for the new item in hand.

When you feel they are ready, instruct the students to draw a picture of something that they own. When the picture is complete, give each child a sentence strip to write a sentence that shows his or her ownership of the item. Allow time for the children to share their pictures and sentences. Display them for all to read.

Punctuation: Quotation Marks

Character Conversations

Activity:

Students will write a conversation for two "characters" in a provided picture.

Materials:

- pictures with two people, animals, or objects (1 per student team)
- writing paper (1 per picture)
- pencils
- large construction paper (1 per picture)
- glue
- chart paper
- marking pen

Preparation:

1. Mount the pictures and the writing paper on construction paper. Place a picture on top and the writing paper below it.
2. Prepare a sample picture and writing for modeling the activity.

Directions:

Discuss the use of quotation marks. Tell the students that quotations marks are used to identify the words said by someone. The first word inside the quotation marks begins with a capital letter. Punctuation marks are placed inside the final quotation marks.

Display a sample picture and have the children offer conversation ideas for the people, animals, or objects in it. Record their ideas on the chart paper, using quotation marks. Then share your completed sample with the students.

Next, have the students choose partners. Distribute the picture-writing paper sheets and have them brainstorm conversation ideas for their pictures. When ready, they can write their conversations. To share their projects, have the children role-play the conversations they wrote, each partner taking a part.

Display the writing for all to enjoy.

"What would you like to talk about?" asked

Farmer Fred.

Peppy Pig hung his head and said, "The

other pigs are making fun of me."

"My goodness, Peppy! Why?" asked

Farmer Fred.

"I don't like the mud," said Peppy.

In the Bag

Activity:

Students will write a sentence with five items in a series, demonstrating their knowledge of commas in a series.

Materials:

- paper lunch bag (1 per student and teacher)
- five small, special items from home
- stapler or tape
- chart paper

- letter to parents (page 126)
- writing paper
- pencils
- marking pen

Preparation:

1. Write each child's name on a bag.
2. Distribute a bag to each student and instruct the class to do the following:
   - Write your name on the bag.
   - Put five items from home inside the bag.
   - Seal the bag.
3. If necessary, prepare a sample bag to show students. Duplicate and distribute a parent letter to each student.

Directions:

Tell the students about using commas in a series. Give them the following information: A comma tells the reader where to pause. For words in a series, put a comma after each item except the last. Do not use a comma if only two items are listed. Also use commas to separate two or more adjectives that are listed together unless one adjective tells how many.

This activity will be managed over two days. On the first day, share with the students the items in your sample bag, naming each item as you remove it from the bag. On the chart paper write, "Five things from home that I like a lot are . . . ." Ask the children to help you to complete the sentence by recalling the five items that were in the bag. While writing, model how to use commas in a series.

Give each child a paper lunch bag and a letter to the parents, explaining that they are to put five small, special items from home into the bag to bring to school the next school day.

On the next day, have each child share his or her five items with a partner or in a small group. Remind the students to name each item as it is removed from the bag. When their sharing is complete, reread for the students the sentence you wrote on the first day. Have the children imitate your sentence, writing their own with their own five items.

Punctuation: Commas in a Series

In the Bag: Parent Letter

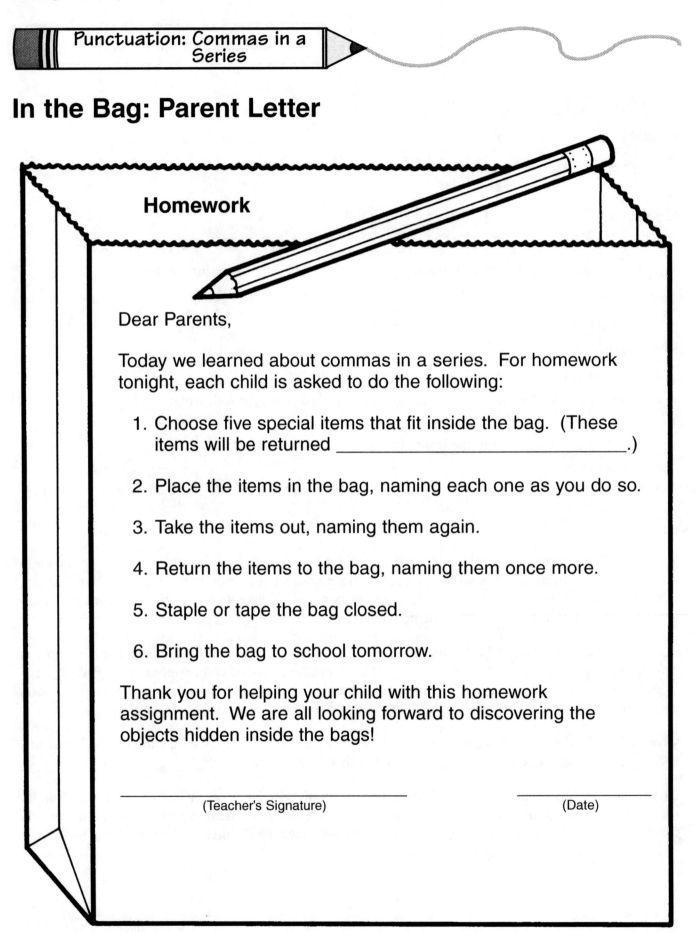

Homework

Dear Parents,

Today we learned about commas in a series. For homework tonight, each child is asked to do the following:

1. Choose five special items that fit inside the bag. (These items will be returned _____.)

2. Place the items in the bag, naming each one as you do so.

3. Take the items out, naming them again.

4. Return the items to the bag, naming them once more.

5. Staple or tape the bag closed.

6. Bring the bag to school tomorrow.

Thank you for helping your child with this homework assignment. We are all looking forward to discovering the objects hidden inside the bags!

_____   _____
(Teacher's Signature)   (Date)

More Parts of Speech

Dyno Detective II

Activity:

Students will become "detectives" to locate various parts of speech.

Materials:

- Dyno Detective notebook Cover on page 44 (1 per child)
- Dyno Detective Poster (page 45)
- task cards (pages 46–48, 128 and 29)
- Dyno Detective Awards (page 49)
- marking pen
- construction paper
- poster board

- writing paper
- stapler
- crayons, markers, or colored pencils
- paper clip
- scissors
- pencils
- laminating machine (optional)

Preparation:

See page 43 for all preparatory information.

Directions:

This is an ongoing activity that "investigates" parts of speech. You will need to decide on the frequency of your investigative sessions as well as their length of time.

Display the Dyno Detective Poster for a few days to pique the children's curiosity. Then gather the children to pass out their Dyno Detective notebooks and to explain the detective process. (Allow the students to write their names on the covers.) Let the students know that a different task card will be inserted in the poster's Special Task section during each detective-work period. Then, choose a task card and attach it to the Dyno Detective Poster. Work with the students to complete this first investigation. Afterwards, let them do their detective work individually or with a partner.

Share the children's investigative work at the end of the allotted time.

In addition to the noun and verb cards provided on pages 46, 47, 128, and 129 offer task cards for pronouns, adjectives, adverbs, possessives, and commas in a series. Page 48 offers blank cards for you to fill in as you choose.

More Parts of Speech

Dyno Detective II Task Cards

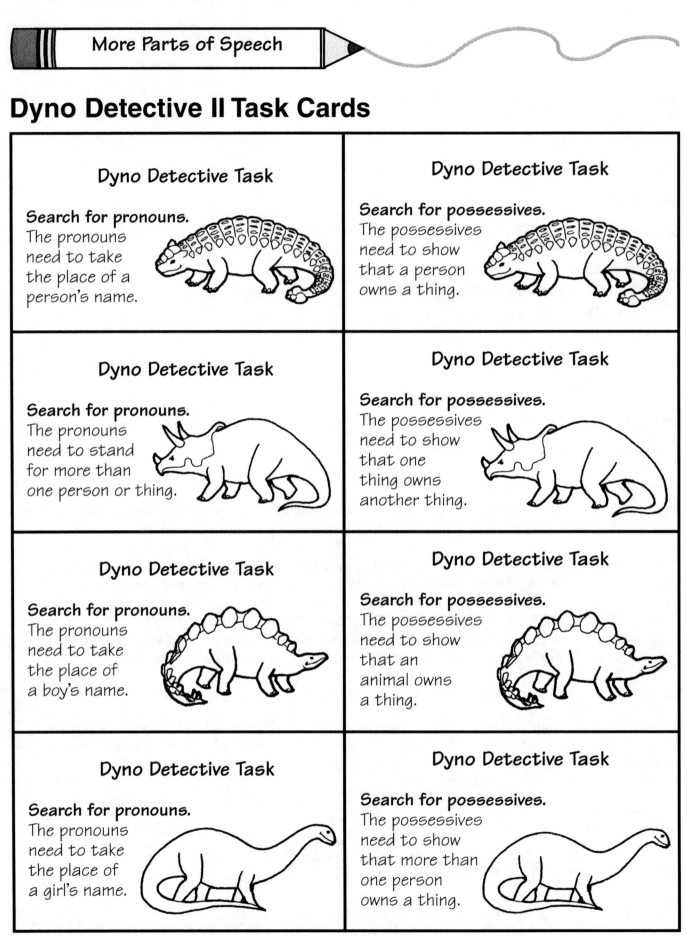

Dyno Detective Task

Search for pronouns.
The pronouns need to take the place of a person's name.

Dyno Detective Task

Search for possessives.
The possessives need to show that a person owns a thing.

Dyno Detective Task

Search for pronouns.
The pronouns need to stand for more than one person or thing.

Dyno Detective Task

Search for possessives.
The possessives need to show that one thing owns another thing.

Dyno Detective Task

Search for pronouns.
The pronouns need to take the place of a boy's name.

Dyno Detective Task

Search for possessives.
The possessives need to show that an animal owns a thing.

Dyno Detective Task

Search for pronouns.
The pronouns need to take the place of a girl's name.

Dyno Detective Task

Search for possessives.
The possessives need to show that more than one person owns a thing.

Dyno Detective II Task Cards *(cont.)*

Dyno Detective Task

Search for adjectives.
The adjectives
need to
describe
dinosaurs.

Dyno Detective Task

Search for adverbs.
The adverbs
need to
tell when.

Dyno Detective Task

Search for adjectives.
The adjectives
need to
describe
stars.

Dyno Detective Task

Search for adverbs.
The adverbs
need to tell
how much.
or how often.

Dyno Detective Task

Search for adjectives.
The adjectives
need to
describe you.

Dyno Detective Task

Search for adverbs.
The adverbs
need to
tell where.

Dyno Detective Task

Search for adjectives.
The adjectives
need to
describe
the earth.

Dyno Detective Task

Search for adverbs.
The adverbs
need to
tell how or why.

Four Writing Genres

- Letter
- Narrative

- Persuasive
- Expository

Letter Writing

Introduction

The ability to write a letter is an important skill that can be taught to primary children. Letters do not need to be lengthy, but they should include all the appropriate parts: heading, greeting, body, closing, and signature.

- The heading includes the date on which the letter is written.
- The greeting includes the name of the person to whom the letter is written, and it is usually preceded with "Dear."
- The body of the letter includes the things being said to the recipient of the letter. This is the "heart" of the letter.
- The closing is an expression of feeling, and the following words and phrases are often used: sincerely, your friend, love, best wishes.
- The signature identifies the author of the letter.

Letter writing is a life skill and should be taught as such. Realistic letter writing opportunities include the following:

- friendly letter
- thank you note
- business request letter
- friendly request letter

Letters can be used to introduce other writing genres as well.

- friendly letter = narrative writing
- friendly request letter = persuasive writing

Write letters often. Write them for fun. Write them to each other. Send them home or put them in the mail. Who knows? The more the students write and send letters, the more likely they are to receive letters in turn, and everyone enjoys that.

Letter Writing

The Friendly Letter: Kindergarten

Activity:

Students will write a friendly letter and draw accompanying pictures.

Materials:

- chart paper
- marking pen
- *The Jolly Postman* by Janet and Allen Ahlberg
- drawing paper
- colored pencils, crayons, or markers
- large envelope
- sticker

Preparation:

Arrange with a staff member (principal, secretary, custodian, etc.) to receive and respond to a friendly letter from your class.

Directions:

The result of this lesson will be a class-composed, friendly letter to a school staff member such as the principal, secretary, or custodian.

Maple Elementary School
22114 Maple Street
Seattle, WA 98055

Attn: Miss Ansley

Begin by introducing the book *The Jolly Postman* and reading one or two of the letters. (Additional letters can be read prior to other letter-writing lessons, if desired.) Discuss with the children the conventions of the letters.

Next, with the teacher doing the writing, the children can compose a letter to the chosen staff member. Write the letter on the chart paper. The letter should include all the parts of a friendly letter. (Teach the parts as you go along.) The letter should also contain statements about the class such as how many children there are, how many boys there are compared to girls, some of the things the children like to do in school, and so forth. Have each child sign the letter at the bottom below the closing.

Each child can then draw a picture related to the letter. Each picture should be labeled and identified.

The letter and pictures should be placed in an envelope and properly addressed, even though it will be hand-delivered. A stamp-sized sticker can be used and placed in the proper place on the envelope.

When the response is received, share it with the class.

The Friendly Letter: First Grade

Activity:

Students will write friendly letters.

Materials:

- overhead projector, transparency, and markers
- chart paper and a marking pen or chalkboard
- *The Jolly Postman* by Janet and Allen Ahlberg
- writing paper (Providing "special" paper encourages the students' interest.)
- pencils
- drawing paper (optional)
- crayons, colored pencils, or markers (optional)
- envelope
- sticker

Preparation:

1. Prepare an overhead transparency of the writing paper the children will use.
2. Arrange with a staff member (principal, secretary, custodian, etc.) to receive and respond to a friendly letter from your class.

Directions:

The result of this lesson will be a student-written, friendly letter to a school staff member such as the principal, secretary, or custodian. Do this lesson early in the year as an introduction to the staff member.

Begin by introducing the book *The Jolly Postman* and reading one or two of the letters (or the entire book if your students will remain attentive). Unread letters can be read prior to other letter-writing lessons.

After reading, have the students brainstorm ideas that could be included in their own letter to the staff member. Record their responses on the chart paper or chalkboard.

As a class, draft a letter. Use the overhead (and the transparency you prepared) to demonstrate writing a letter that includes all the parts. Emphasize each part as you write it, its purpose as well as its location in the letter. The body of the letter should include a question that can be responded to by the letter's recipient.

After the class letter is complete, give each student a copy of the special writing paper and have students compose their own letters, using the information on the chart paper. Their letters do not need to be lengthy, but they should include all components of a friendly letter. Send all the letters to the recipient. Be sure to address the envelope correctly, even though the letter will be hand-delivered. A stamp-sized sticker can be used and placed in the proper place on the envelope.

Please note that although many letters will be sent, the recipient is not expected to respond to each student individually. One letter to the class as a whole will suffice.

If desired, self-portraits can be included with the letters when they are sent.

When the response is received, share it with the class.

Letter Writing

The Friendly Letter: Second and Third Grade

Activity:

Students will write friendly letters.

Materials:

- overhead projector, transparencies, and markers
- chart paper and marking pen
- *The Jolly Postman* by Janet and Allen Ahlberg
- writing paper (Providing "special" paper encourages the students' interest.)
- drawing paper (optional)
- colored pencils, crayons, or markers (optional)
- envelopes
- stickers

Preparation:

1. Prepare an overhead transparency of the writing paper the children will use.

2. Have each student arrange with a staff member (principal, secretary, custodian, other teacher, etc.) to receive and respond to a friendly letter which he or she will write.

Directions:

The result of this lesson will be a student-composed, friendly letter to a school staff member such as the principal, secretary, or custodian. Do this lesson early in the year as an introduction to the staff member.

Begin by introducing the book *The Jolly Postman* and reading one or two of the letters (or the entire book if your students are likely to remain attentive). Unread letters can be read prior to other letter-writing lessons.

Have the children brainstorm ideas that could be included in the letter. Record their responses on chart paper or the chalkboard.

Use the overhead (and the transparency you prepared) to demonstrate writing a letter which includes all the parts. Emphasize each part as you write it, including its purpose and location in the letter. The body of the letter should include a question that can be responded to by the letter's recipient.

After you have drafted a letter as a class, instruct each child to compose his or her own letter, using ideas from the chart paper and others of his or her own. Allow the students to use the special writing paper for their letters. Letters should include several sentences in the body and all the parts of a friendly letter. A picture related to the body of the letter or a self-portrait can be added to the letter.

Each letter and picture should be placed in an envelope and addressed properly even though it will be hand-delivered. A stamp-sized sticker can be affixed in the proper place on the envelope.

When the students receive their responses, allow them to share them with the class.

Giant Letter

Activity:

Students will construct a friendly letter and label its parts.

Materials:

- sheet of brightly-colored bulletin board paper
- marking pen
- sentence strips

Preparation:

Prepare the bulletin board paper by cutting it to the desired size.

Directions:

Review the parts of a letter with the students. As a class, construct a simple letter. Write the letter on the bulletin board paper, using the correct letter format.

When complete, choral read the letter.

Write the names of the various parts of a letter on individual sentence strips. Attach the sentence strips to the "giant letter" in the appropriate locations. Display the letter and sentence strips in a prominent location for the children to use as a reference when writing a friendly letter.

September 1, 1998

Dear Mrs. Cross,

We enjoyed your visit to our classroom. Thank you for taking the time to talk with us. Please come again!

Your friends,
The Children of
Room 12

Letter Writing

Pen Pals: Kindergarten

Activity:

Students will compose a pen-pal letter to a neighboring school.

Materials:

- teacher's name and school address from another same-grade class
- student names from the same class (1 per student)
- writing paper
- chart paper
- marking pen
- individual or class photographs
- large envelope
- postage

Preparation:

Contact a same-grade teacher at another school in your district or a neighboring district to arrange a pen-pal project.

Directions:

Discuss the concept of pen pals with the children. Also discuss the things the children would like to tell children in another kindergarten class. Record their responses on chart paper.

Next, discuss the things the children would like to know about children in another kindergarten class. Record their responses on chart paper.

Using the correct form for a friendly letter, have the children compose a class letter to the pen-pal class at the other school. Record their letter on the chart paper.

When the letter is complete, read it in unison. Have each of the children sign his or her name at the bottom under the closing. Attach an individual photograph next to each signature or include a class photograph with each child's picture identified so the other children will be able to match a name with a face.

Address the envelope, insert the letter, add postage, and mail it. When you receive a response, share it with the class and write another letter in return. Continue the correspondence throughout the year, meeting the other class at some point for a big group picnic.

Letter Writing

Pen Pals: First, Second, and Third Grades

Activity:

Students will each compose a pen-pal letter to a student at a neighboring school.

Materials:

- teacher's name and school address from another same-grade class
- student names from the same class (1 per student)
- chart paper
- marking pen

- writing paper
- pencils
- individual photographs
- envelopes
- postage

Preparation:

Contact a same-grade teacher at another school in your district or a neighboring district to arrange a pen-pal project.

Directions:

Discuss the concept of pen pals with the children. Share with them the arrangements you made with the first or second grade children at the other school.

As a class, discuss the things the children would like to tell the children in the other class. Record their responses on chart paper. Then discuss the things the children would like to know about the children in the other class. Record their responses on chart paper.

Walk the children through the correct form for a friendly letter. Allow each student to write the body of his or her own letter, using the format and the ideas on the chart paper.

When the letters are complete, have the children share them with a partner. They should then revise and edit their letters, as necessary.

Provide each child with a photograph to attach to the bottom of his or her letter. Have each child address an envelope, insert the letter and photograph, add postage, and mail it.

When the students receive responses to their letters, allow them to share them with the class. Continue your pen-pal correspondence through the year, getting together for a group picnic at some point so that the students can meet one another face to face.

Letter Writing

The Thank You Note: Class

Activity:

Students will write a class thank you note.

Materials:

- chart paper
- pencil
- postage
- marking pen
- drawing paper
- colored pencils, crayons, or markers
- writing paper
- large envelope

Preparation:

Select a person or organization whom the class can thank, such as the bus driver for your last field trip or a parent helper.

Directions:

This will serve as a demonstration lesson for the writing of individual thank you notes.

To begin, tell the students that thank you notes should contain statements about the things for which they are thankful. They should also express gratitude. With that in mind, have the children brainstorm ideas that can be included in their thank you note. Write their ideas on the chart paper.

With the teacher doing the writing, let the children compose the thank you note. Again, use chart paper. The note should include all standard parts of a friendly letter. Be sure to point out the necessity for these parts as you and the students write.

When the letter is complete, allow each child to draw a picture related to the letter. Each picture should be labeled and identified.

Place the letter and pictures in an envelope, address it properly, add postage, and mail the letter.

Letter Writing

The Thank You Note: Individual

Activity:

Each student will compose a thank you note.

Materials:

- overhead projector, transparency, and markers
- chart paper and marking pen
- note paper (patterns, pages 140 and 141)
- pencils
- crayons, colored pencils, or markers (optional)
- envelopes
- postage

Preparation:

1. Prepare an overhead transparency of the writing paper the children will use.
2. Have the students bring in the name and address for someone to whom they can write a thank you note.

Directions:

Ask each child to select an individual for whom it would be appropriate to write a thank you note. Have the children brainstorm ideas that could be included in their thank you notes. Record their responses on chart paper. (See additional information on page 138.)

Give the children a word bank of names such as grandma, grandpa, aunt, uncle, Mr. _____, Mrs. _____, Mom, Dad, and so forth. This will help them with their future letter writing, as well.

Model for the class the writing of a thank you note. Use the overhead transparency of the same writing paper they will use for their notes.

Next, allow the children to compose their own thank you notes, using the ideas from the chart paper and the overhead transparency to guide them. The note should include a heading, a greeting, a sentence in the body that states that for which the writer is thankful (as well as expressing his/her gratitude), a closing, and the writer's signature. A picture related to the body of the note can be added, if desired.

All thank you notes should be placed in envelopes, addressed, stamped, and mailed. However, if all the notes are written to the same person, they can be placed in one envelope and mailed together, or if the notes are addressed to the students' parents, allow them to draw stamps on their envelopes and hand-deliver their letters.

Letter Writing

The Thank You Note: Stationery A

Letter Writing

The Thank You Note: Stationery B

Letter Writing

The Business Request Letter: Kindergarten

Activity:

The class will write and send a business request letter.

Materials:

- chart paper
- marking pen
- large envelope
- postage

Preparation:

No preparation is required.

Directions:

The result of this lesson will be a class-composed letter to request specific information from a business.

Have the children brainstorm for a topic about which they would like to learn more. This can be anything from butterflies to amusement parks. Vote as a class for the topic you most want to investigate.

Next, discuss which people or organizations might have information to share about that topic. Choose one of those people/organizations to whom you will write your class letter.

With the teacher doing the actual writing, the children can compose the letter requesting the specific information. The letter should include all standard parts of a letter. Be sure to point out these parts as you write. Particularly point out the greeting which is traditionally written "Dear Sir or Madam," and is usually followed by a colon. If an actual name is known, it is written instead of Sir or Madam.

Unlike the previous letters, no pictures are included with this letter. It is much more formal than the other ones.

The letter should be placed in an envelope, addressed properly, stamped, and mailed. It is hoped that the class will receive a response. When they do, share the information received.

Encourage students to continue to write business request letters on their own. Such people and organizations can be valuable resources.

Extension:

When the requested information is received, the class can create a presentation report of the material.

The Business Request Letter: First, Second, and Third Graders

Activity:

Students will write business request letters both as a class and individually.

Materials:

- chart paper
- pencils
- marking pen
- envelopes
- writing paper
- postage

Preparations:

No preparation is required.

Directions (Class):

As a class, brainstorm for the things the students would like to know more about. This list can be wide and varied, including such diverse topics as dinosaurs, chicken pox, and nutrition. As they brainstorm, record their ideas on chart paper. Vote for the topic the class would most like to pursue.

Now the students will need to determine at least three people or organizations who can provide information about that topic. Once sources are selected, locate the correct addresses.

Taking another sheet of chart paper, compose (as a class) a business letter of request, asking for some specific information. The letter should include all standard parts of a letter. Be sure to point out these parts as you write. Particularly point out the greeting which is traditionally written "Dear Sir or Madam" and is usually followed by a colon. If an actual name is known, it is written instead of Sir or Madam.

When complete, choral read the letter. Revise and edit as necessary. Unlike the previous letters, no pictures are included with this letter. It is much more formal than the other ones.

Make as many copies of this letter as needed onto regular writing paper. Place each letter in an envelope, address it properly, stamp it, and mail all of them. It is hoped that the class will receive responses. When the responses come, share the information received.

Encourage students to continue to write business request letters on their own. Such people and organizations can be valuable resources. End-of-the-year second graders and third graders should be able to do this on their own after the modeling done as a class.

Directions (Individual):

Each child will write a business letter requesting information about a specific topic of the child's choice. As a class, brainstorm for topics and sources, and then let each child choose his or her own. Help them to gather the correct addresses for mailing.

First, model for the students the correct business letter form and then allow each student to compose his or her own letter. Take the letters through the writing process, getting peer responses, revising, editing, and finally making a final, neat copy. The letters should be addressed and mailed. Share responses when they are received.

Letter Writing

The Friendly Letter: First, Second, and Third Grades

Activity:

Students will write individual letters of request to their parents.

Materials:

- 3 colors of writing paper
- pencils
- glue
- envelopes
- scissors
- white writing paper
- postage

Preparation:

1. Prepare and display the proper friendly letter form for the students' reference.
2. Prepare the 3 colors of writing paper as follows: 1st color = full sheet, 2nd/3rd colors = partial sheets.

Directions:

These letters will take the form of a persuasive letter containing a topic sentence, three sentences of support, and a restatement of the topic sentence. These letters can be written to a parent(s) or another individual from whom such a request is appropriate (for example, Santa Claus).

Have each child think of something he or she would like to receive for a special occasion such as a birthday, Christmas, or Hanukkah. Let them share their ideas with the class.

As a class, review the major components of friendly letters. Remind the students that they will need to use all parts in their letters.

The letters themselves can be composed in the following manner (to help the students organize their letters and to include all necessary information): Children begin their letters on full-sized sheets of writing paper (first color). This sheet should include the heading and the greeting. Next, each child writes a topic sentence, stating the name of the item he or she would like to receive. This should be written on the second colored paper, and each child should write this sentence twice. On the third colored paper, the child writes three supporting sentences, each one stating a reason why he or she would like/should have this item. Challenge the students not to use the word "because" in these sentences. Offer them alternatives.

When the letters are complete, put them together in this manner:

1. Take the full sheet of paper with the heading and greeting.
2. Glue one of the topic sentences under the greeting.
3. Glue the three supporting sentences under the topic sentence.
4. Glue the second copy of the topic sentence under the support sentences.
5. Add the closing and signature.

When the letters are organized, have students copy their letters onto good writing paper, address the envelopes, add stamps, and mail the letters.

Note: Have the students develop their "arguments" according to their ability levels.

144

The Friendly Letter: Kindergarten

Activity:

Students will write a friendly business letter from the class.

Materials:

- candy bar or wrapper (1 per student)
- marking pen
- postage
- chart paper
- large envelope

Preparation:

Instruct each child to bring in a favorite candy bar or candy bar wrapper.

Directions:

Have each child bring his or her favorite candy bar or candy bar wrapper to school. (Many math activities can be done with these before or after the letter writing experience.) Make a list of the different candy bars the children bring and the names and addresses of the companies that make them. (Most are listed on the wrappers of the candy bars). Determine the most popular candy bar.

Have the children brainstorm the reasons they like this (or any other) candy bar. Record their responses on the chart paper.

With the children dictating, and using the correct form for a friendly business letter, compose a class letter to the company. Write the letter on chart paper. Include reasons the children like the candy bar and how many chose it as their favorite. Finally, request a sample of the candy for the class.

When the letter is complete, choral read it. Have each of the children sign it. Address the envelope, add postage, and mail the letter.

When a response is received, share it with the class.

Notes:

A friendly business letter of request differs from a business letter of request in that it contains personal information in addition to a request.

A good time to do this activity is just after Halloween if the children in your class participate in trick-or-treat activities.

This letter writing activity can be done with almost any food item that is not perishable.

Letter Writing

The Friendly Letter: First, and Second, and Third Grades

Activity:

Students will write a friendly business letter from the class.

Materials:

- candy bar or wrapper (1 per student)
- marking pen
- pencils
- postage

- chart paper
- writing paper
- envelopes

Preparation:

Instruct each child to bring in a favorite candy bar or candy bar wrapper.

Directions:

Have each child bring his or her favorite candy bar or candy bar wrapper to school. (Many math activities can be done with these before or after the letter writing experience.) Make a list of the different candy bars the children bring and the names and addresses of the companies that make them. (Most are listed on the wrapper of the candy bar). Determine the most popular candy bar.

Have the children brainstorm the reasons they like this (or any other) candy bar. Record their responses on the chart paper.

Guide the students in brainstorming for items that should be included in their letters.

- the name of their favorite candy bar
- reasons it is their favorite candy bar
- request for a sample of the candy

Give each child a piece of writing paper. Model the correct form for the beginning of a friendly business letter while the children follow along on their own writing paper. Then have each child write the body of his or her letter individually. When the students are ready, partner them for a peer conference. Instruct them to revise and then edit as necessary.

Provide each child with an envelope which should be addressed to the candy company, the letter inserted, postage added, and the letter mailed.

Notes:

A friendly business letter of request differs from a business letter of request in that it contains personal information in addition to a request.

A good time to do this activity is just after Halloween if the children in your class participate in trick-or-treat activities.

This letter writing activity can be done with almost any food item that is not perishable.

Parts-of-a-Letter Poster

Attach pages 148–150 as shown. If desired, let the students color the poster and then laminate it for durability. Display it during all your letter writing activities.

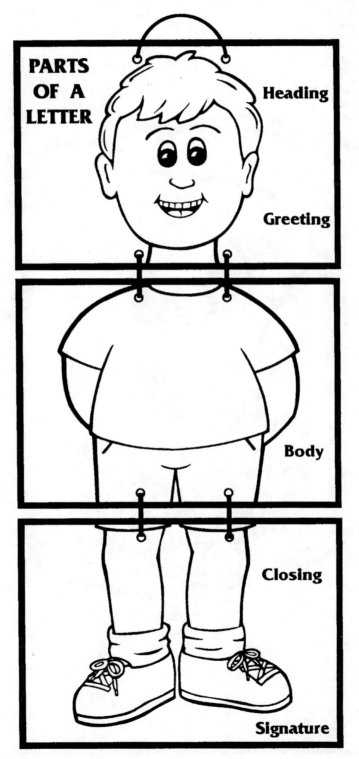

Letter Writing

Parts-of-a-Letter Poster *(cont.)*

Letter Writing

Parts-of-a-Letter Poster *(cont.)*

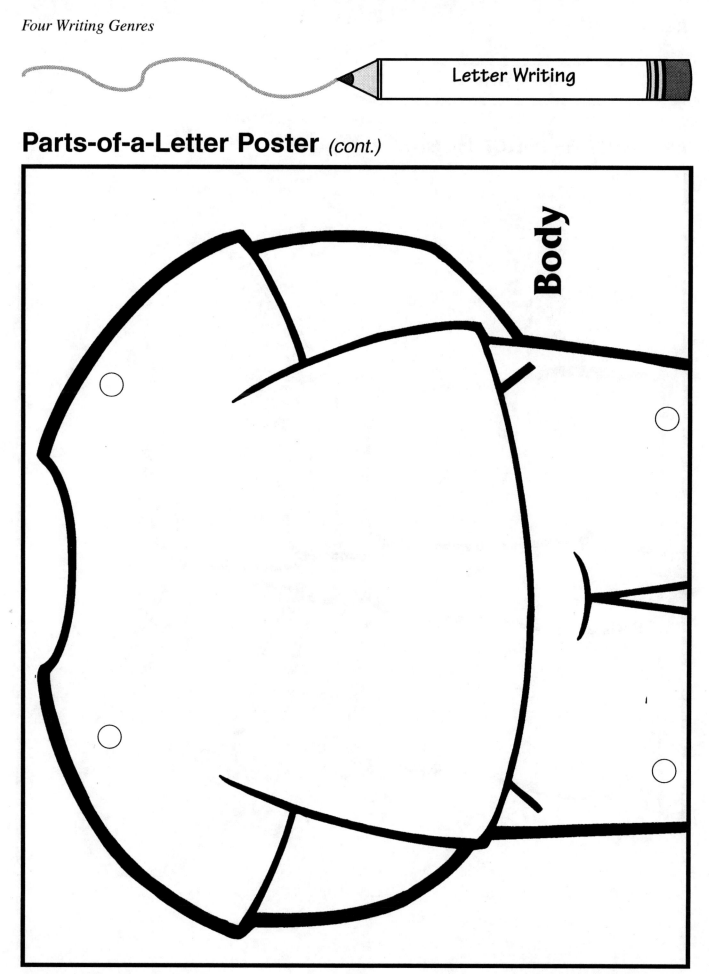

Body

Letter Writing

Parts-of-a-Letter Poster *(cont.)*

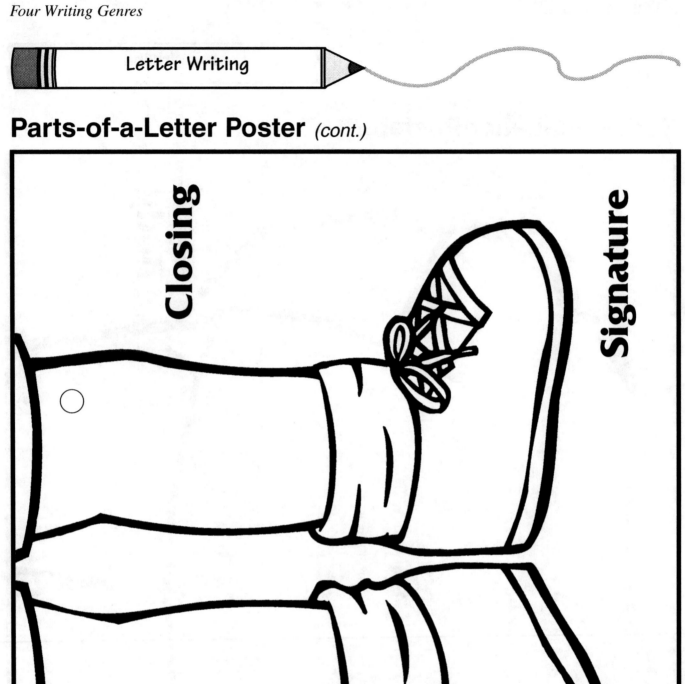

Writing a Paragraph

Activity:

Students will write a paragraph as a precursor to writing a story (page 152).

Materials:

- chart paper
- marking pen
- pencils
- previously completed art project (1 per student and teacher)
- writing paper (1 per student)

Preparation:

Have the students complete an art project or use one they have previously done. Complete one yourself so that you have a model.

Directions:

Show the children your completed art project. Have several children offer one sentence each that tells about your art project. Record their sentences on chart paper.

Take the recorded information and use it as the basis for a paragraph. Model for the students the writing of a paragraph, providing them with the following information:

- A paragraph is a group of sentences with one topic idea.
- A paragraph begins with an indentation on a new line.
- A paragraph consists of a topic sentence and three to five supporting sentences.

Write your paragraph with the students' help. Begin by indenting the first line and writing a topic sentence that tells what you created. For example, "I drew a picture of myself reading a book in the library." Add sentences from the chart paper to expand upon your topic.

When the paragraph is complete, instruct the students to choral read it.

Next, divide the students into partner teams. Ask them to share their art projects with their partners, telling the partners all about their own projects as well as what they see in their partners' projects.

When the sharing is complete, give the children writing paper and have each write a paragraph about his or her art project. Share the completed art projects and paragraphs with the class.

Note: You may wish to have additional practice writing a paragraph before going on to the next activity. It may prove useful to focus on the paragraphs being narrative so that each one tells a short, personal story. For example, a narrative paragraph to go with the sample sentence above might be written like this: "I love to read. One of my favorite things to do is to go to the library on a rainy day. Browsing through the long shelves, I find several books that I might enjoy reading. There are tables in my library, so I take the books to an empty one and I leaf through them, reading a few paragraphs and looking at the pictures. In the library, surrounded by books, I feel cozy and content while the rain falls outside."

Narrative Writing

Writing a Narrative Story

Activity:

The class will write a narrative story.

Materials:

- Narrative Writing Web (page 153; enlarged on chart paper, overhead transparency, or chalkboard)
- chart paper
- marking pen

Preparation:

Create an experience for the children such as going on a field trip, raising butterflies, taking a tour of the school, completing a memorable art project, or watching an interesting nature video.

Directions:

To be narrative writers, the students are asked to tell a story or to describe a series of events in chronological order. In a personal narrative, the author tells about a personal experience, describing the event and his or her reactions or feelings toward what happened. In narrative writing as a whole, any story can be told.

The primary features of personal narrative writing are

- a first-person point of view (I, we).
- chronological organization (events unfold as they happen).
- the significance of the events is revealed.
- the reader shares the writer's thoughts and feelings.

The primary features of narrative writing on the whole are

- the setting (time and place) are clear.
- the characters are developed.
- a problem, conflict, or disagreement motivates the characters.
- the story progresses through a series of events.
- the problem is solved (solution).

All narrative writing should

- state the purpose and topic.
- describe the people, places, and events.
- describe exactly what happened.
- describe what was seen, heard, and felt.

After a common experience, have the students brainstorm the various aspects of the experience. Teach the children how to use the Narrative Writing Web by recording their responses on the enlarged web. Using the completed web for ideas, have the children compose the story, telling about their common experience. Write their story on chart paper. When complete, read the story aloud. Go through each element of narrative writing to be sure that it has been included.

Display the story for future reference and reading practice. Repeat this lesson often before asking the students to write individual stories based on this model. When they are ready, offer them the guidelines for narrative writing and a writing web and have them write and share their own narratives.

Narrative Writing

Narrative Writing Web

Name: _____

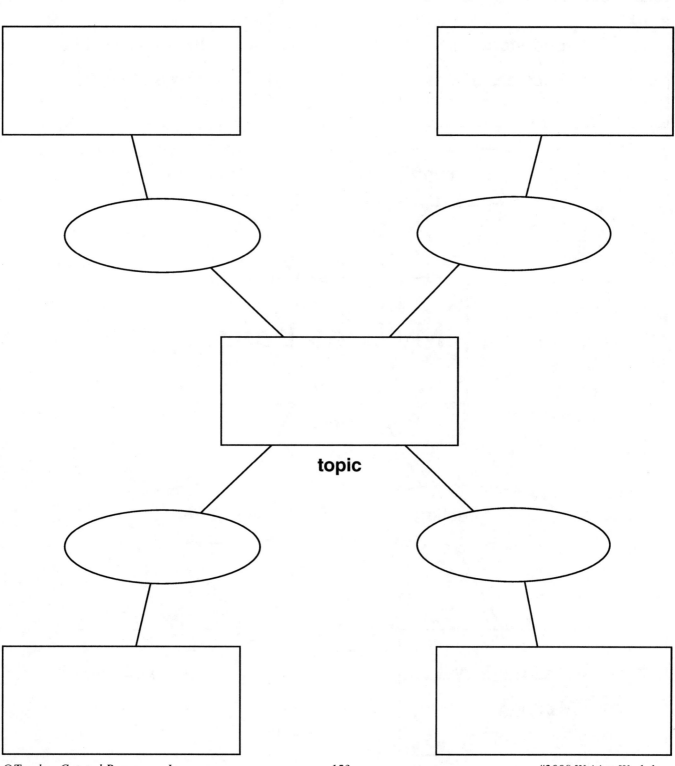

topic

Narrative Writing

Sample Narrative Writing Web

Name: _____

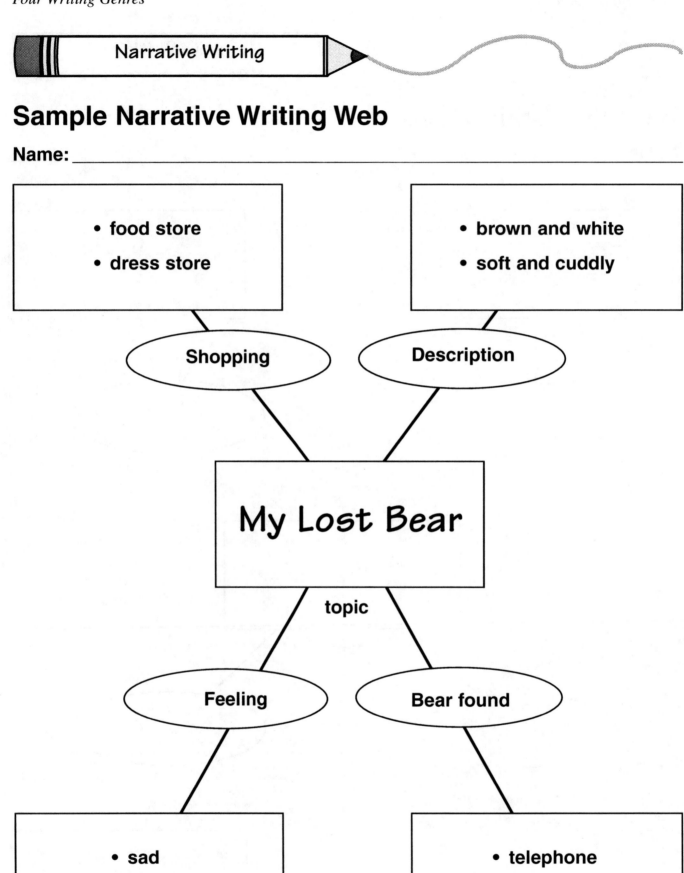

food store
• dress store

Shopping

brown and white
• soft and cuddly

Description

My Lost Bear

topic

Feeling

Bear found

sad
• crying

telephone
• saleslady

Writing a Persuasive Piece

Activity:

The class will compose a persuasive writing piece.

Materials:

- Persuasive Writing Web (page 159, 1 per student)
- Persuasive Writing Web (enlarged on chart paper, overhead transparency, or chalkboard)
- Persuasive Writing Worksheet (page 161, 1 per student)
- Persuasive Writing Worksheet (enlarged on chart paper, overhead, or chalkboard)
- chart paper
- marking pen
- pencils

Preparation:

Select a topic that can be debated and is important to the children, such as getting a (classroom) pet or having an extended recess.

Directions:

Since this is a difficult genre, the children should experience a great deal of modeling and practice creating Persuasive Writing Webs before actually writing a piece of their own.

This type of writing attempts to convince the reader that a point of view is valid or to persuade the reader to take a specific action. Persuasive pieces should be developed around a limited topic that is debatable and meaningful or important. The topic should be one to which students can bring specific evidence and supportable generalization, not just personal opinion or broad generalization.

A persuasive piece should have a topic sentence, three sentences of support (reasons) or elaboration (examples), and a restatement of the topic sentence.

Explain to the students that it is important to have reasons to support opinions. Reasons tell why the reader should agree with the writer. Reasons should offer solid evidence to support the writer's position. The writer can make the reasons more convincing by supporting them with examples.

This activity should be managed differently for kindergartners and for first and second graders. The remainder of the directions are divided accordingly.

Kindergarten

Set the scene for writing by reading a story related to the topic or by discussing the topic. Allow the students to reach a consensus about the topic.

Have the children brainstorm ideas that might convince others that their position is a good one. Use the Persuasive Writing Web to record their ideas. Then compose the persuasive argument as a class, showing the students how to give supports and elaboration in the writing.

When it is complete, read and reread the piece. Display it for future reference and reading practice. Kindergarten children should continue to write class-created pieces throughout the year.

Persuasive Writing

Writing a Persuasive Piece *(cont.)*

First, Second, and Third Grades

Set the scene for writing by reading a story related to the topic or discussing the topic. Have the children brainstorm ideas that might convince others that their position is a good one.

Teach the children how to use a Persuasive Writing Web by recording their responses on an enlarged copy.

Using the Persuasive Writing Web for ideas, complete the Persuasive Writing Worksheet while the children provide the information. The children should give the support and elaboration.

When the worksheet is complete, guide the students in composing the piece. Be sure they include their supports and elaboration using complete sentences and remaining consistent in their arguments.

Repeat this lesson often before asking the children to write individual persuasive pieces based on this model. You might have the students work in small groups and/or partner groups to practice creating a Persuasive Writing Web and Worksheet many times before asking them to compose a piece individually. The web and worksheet are the keys to a well-written piece.

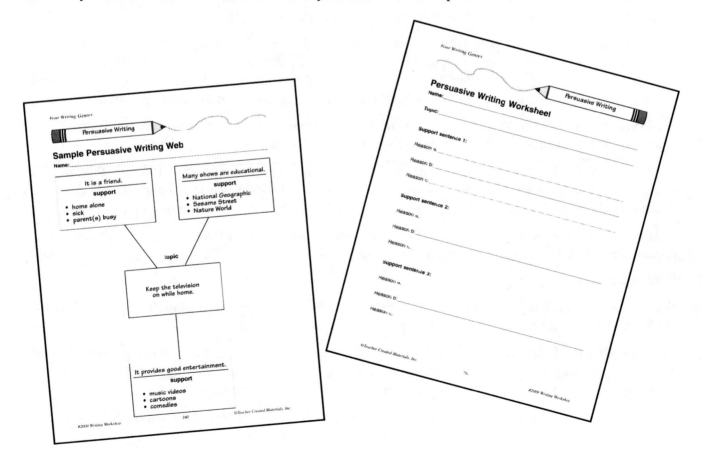

Individual Persuasive Writing Piece: Emergent Writers

Activity:

Students will each write a persuasive piece.

Materials:

- Persuasive Writing Web (page 159)
- white paper
- pencils
- glue
- colored writing paper (2 colors)
- writing paper
- scissors

Preparation:

Have the students practice selecting a persuasive topic and completing a Persuasive Writing Web. The children should begin by working in a small group, advance to working with a partner, and conclude by working individually. This should be done, of course, over many days and weeks. The students should have a great deal of practice writing topics and webs before they are asked to write a persuasive piece on their own.

Directions:

When you feel the class is ready, ask each child to select a topic and to complete a corresponding web. Then, have them do the following:

1. Write the topic sentence twice on one color of writing paper.

2. Write three supporting sentences on the other color of writing paper.

3. Glue the sentences onto the white paper in this order: one topic sentence, three support sentences, one topic sentence.

The students can recopy their sentences onto clean writing paper. When the activity is complete, have them share their persuasive arguments with the class.

Persuasive Writing

Individual Persuasive Writing Piece: Fluent Writer

Activity:

Students will each write a persuasive piece.

Materials:

- Persuasive Writing Web (page 159)
- colored writing paper (3 colors)
- writing paper
- scissors
- Persuasive Writing Worksheet (page 161)
- white paper
- pencils
- glue

Preparation:

Have the students practice selecting a persuasive topic, completing a Persuasive Writing Web, and completing a Persuasive Writing Worksheet. The children should begin by working in a small group, advancing to working with a partner, and then to working individually. This should be done, of course, over many days and weeks. The students should have a great deal of practice writing topics, webs, and worksheets before they are asked to write a persuasive piece on their own.

Directions:

When you feel the class is ready, ask each child to select a topic and to complete a corresponding web and worksheet. Then, have them do the following:

---

1. Write the main topic sentence twice on one color of writing paper.

2. Write support sentences 1, 2, and 3 on the second color of writing paper.

3. Write the three reason sentences for each on the third color of writing paper.

4. Glue the sentences onto the plain paper in this order: one main topic sentence, support sentence 1, three reason sentences for support of sentence 1, support sentence 2, three reason sentences for support of sentence 2, support sentence 3, three reason sentences for support of sentence 3, and the remaining main topic sentence.

The students should then recopy their sentences onto clean writing paper. When the sentences are complete, have the students share their persuasive arguments with the class.

Persuasive Writing

Persuasive Writing Web

Name:_____

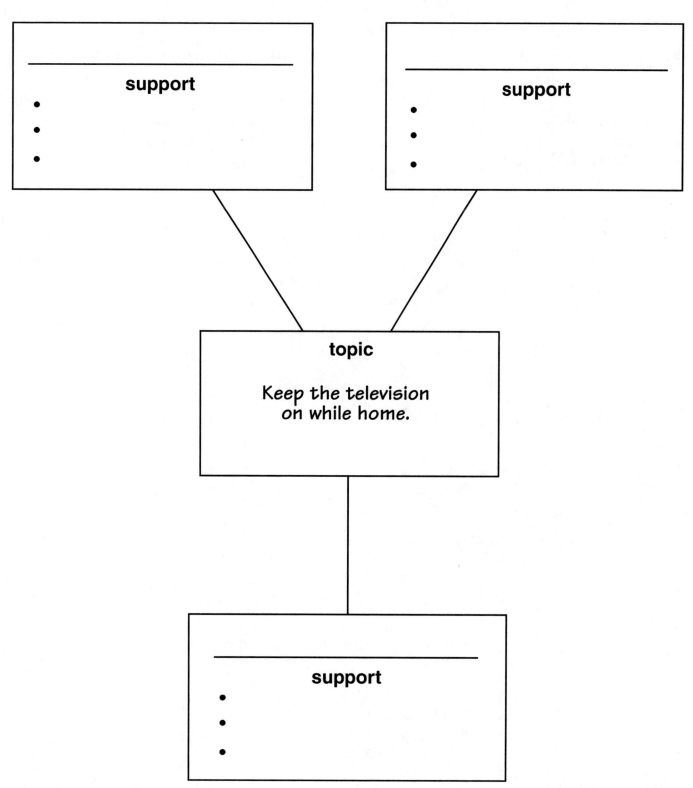

support

- •
- •
- •

support

- •
- •
- •

topic

Keep the television
on while home.

support

- •
- •
- •

Persuasive Writing

Sample Persuasive Writing Web

Name:_____

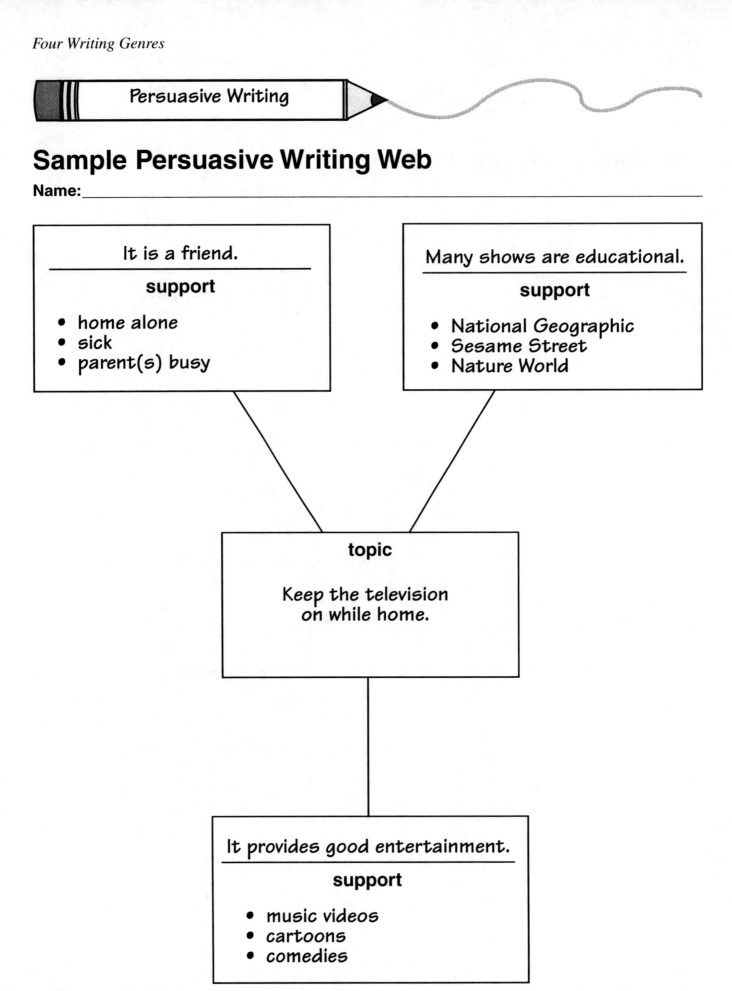

It is a friend.
_____
support

- home alone
- sick
- parent(s) busy

Many shows are educational.
_____
support

- *National Geographic*
- *Sesame Street*
- *Nature World*

topic

Keep the television
on while home.

It provides good entertainment.
_____
support

- music videos
- cartoons
- comedies

Persuasive Writing

Persuasive Writing Worksheet

Name:_____ **Topic:**_____

Support sentence 1:_____

_____

Reason a: _____

Reason b: _____

Reason c: _____

Support sentence 2:_____

_____

Reason a: _____

Reason b: _____

Reason c: _____

Support sentence 3:_____

_____

Reason a: _____

Reason b: _____

Reason c: _____

Persuasive Writing

Sample Persuasive Writing Worksheet

Name:_____

Topic: Our school is the best school in town.

Support sentence 1: The teachers are very helpful.

Reason a: The teachers are at school before it starts so that they can help the students.

Reason b: The teachers stay after school to help the students with their homework.

Reason c: The teachers encourage the students to ask questions when they do not understand.

Support sentence 2: The principal at our school is involved with the children.

Reason a: Every day the principal visits every classroom in our school to talk with the children.

Reason b: The principal eats lunch with each child once during the year.

Reason c: Our principal participates in our field day activities.

Support sentence 3: Our classrooms are very well equipped.

Reason a: Every classroom has math manipulatives such as pattern blocks and geoboards.

Reason b: All the classrooms have two computers and programs about math and reading.

Reason c: Each classroom has a library with books that can be checked out by the students.

Persuasive Writing Topics

1. Our school is the best school in town.

2. Tourists should visit my state/province.

3. Small children should always be supervised.

4. You must read _____.

5. My mom makes the best blueberry muffins in the world.

6. Every child should have good handwriting.

7. Every toddler needs a teddy bear of his or her own.

8. The _____ County Fair promises a fun-filled time for everyone.

9. The _____ is the best looking car on the road.

10. _____ should be our student council representative.

11. _____ should be our student council president.

12. Bike riders should wear helmets.

13. The school year should be longer.

14. _____ is the best television show.

15. _____ is the worst television show.

16. _____ is the hardest subject in school.

17. Families should turn off their television one night every week.

18. Families should have "family night" every week.

19. Family members should take turns choosing the activity for "family night" each week.

20. People should not litter.

21. Our school needs more _____.

22. Everybody should have a garden.

23. _____ is the best sport.

24. Everyone should wear seatbelts.

25. The best thing about school is _____.

Expository Writing

Writing a Class Expository Piece

Activity:

The class will compose an expository writing piece.

Materials:

- Expository Writing Notes (page 175; enlarged on chart paper, overhead transparency, or chalkboard)
- Expository Writing Web 1 (page 176; enlarged on chart paper, overhead transparency, or chalkboard)
- chart paper
- marking pen
- several books on a selected topic

Preparation:

Select a topic to write about that is important to the children. Collect several books on the topic.

Directions:

This type of writing gives information, describes or explains something, or defines the meaning of something. Expository pieces may be developed by comparison-contrast, with facts and statistics, through examples, by cause and effect, and/or by definitions. The expository piece is usually unemotional and is written in the third person.

Expository writing should

- state the purpose and topic.
- explain.
- include facts, give reasons, and/or give examples.

Set the scene for writing by reading and discussing your selected books over a period of days. Then lead the students in brainstorming things they have learned about the topic. Model taking notes by recording their responses on the enlarged copy of Expository Writing Notes (page 175), grouping similar information.

Teach the children how to use the Expository Writing Web 1 on page 176 by transferring their responses to the enlarged web. Then using the web for ideas, guide the students in composing a class expository piece, giving facts and examples to tell about the topic.

When it is complete, read and reread the piece. Hang the piece for future reference and reading practice.

Repeat this lesson often before asking first and second grade students to write individual expository pieces based on this model. Kindergarten children should continue to write class-composed pieces throughout the year.

Writing a Small Group/Individual Expository Piece

Activity:

Each small group or student will compose an expository report.

Materials:

- Expository Writing Notes (page 175)
- nonfiction picture books
- pencils
- Expository Writing Web 1 (page 176)
- writing paper

Preparation:

Determine a research topic or topics for the students. If desired, allow the class to determine the topic(s).

Directions:

This activity should be managed differently, depending on the skill level of the students.

- ### Beginning Writers

  Have the students work in small groups to gather information from pictures in nonfiction picture books. They can write the information on the Expository Writing Web 1 on page 176, grouping similar information together. Provide them with a frame sentence and instruct them to use it to write several sentences with the web information. (If desired, let beginning writers make notes on the Idea Graph for Beginning Writers, page 180.)

- ### Emerging Writers

  Have the students work with a partner to complete an expository report. Tell them to read (or have read to them) at least two nonfiction picture books on the topic. They will record the information they learn on the Expository Writing Notes on page 175, grouping similar information together. The information can be organized and transferred to the Expository Writing Web 1. From this, they will write sentences, using the ideas from the web.

- ### Fluent Writers

  The students will work individually to complete an expository report. They will need to read several nonfiction sources to gather information about the topic. The information should be recorded on the Expository Writing Notes, grouping similar information together. These ideas are then organized and transferred to the Expository Writing Web 1. From this, they will write sentences to create an expository report.

Expository Writing

How To

Activity:

Each small group or student will compose an expository piece that explains "how to."

Materials:

- Expository Writing Web 2 (page 178)
- pencils
- crayons
- writing paper
- drawing paper

Preparation:

Determine a "how to" topic or topics for the students. If desired, allow the class to determine the topic(s). Telling how to do something includes a wide variety of possibilities. For example: How do you make popcorn? How do you stop a nosebleed? How do you get to the store? Have the students write about something they have personally learned or experienced.

Directions:

Remind the students that expository writing is to be explicit. When explaining "how to," the writing must include every step (as in a recipe).

Sequence is important. Sequencing words that can be used in this type of expository writing include *first* (second, etc.), *then, after, next, last*, and *finally*. You may wish to spend some time with the students brainstorming for additional sequence words.

The rest of this activity should be managed differently, depending on the skill level of the students.

- **Beginning Writers**

  The entire class can work in small groups on the same topic. Children may begin by drawing pictures of the various steps involved in the activity. The steps are then written on the Expository Writing Web 2 (page 178). Then, each group writes several sentences with the information from the web. When it is complete, the writing should be published.

- **Emerging Writers**

  Children work with a partner. First, each team completes the Expository Writing Web 2, including all the steps involved in the activity. The teams then write sentences, using the ideas on the web. When it is complete, the piece is published.

- **Fluent Writers**

  Children work individually. The Expository Writing Web 2 is completed first. Then the information is transferred from the web in sentence form to create an expository piece.

  Finally, the piece is published in one of the following ways:

  — individual books

  — a class book

  — posters

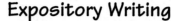

Expository Writing

Let's Pretend (Kindergarten)

Activity:

Each student will write about an occupation. The class will make an occupations book.

Materials:

- *Let's Pretend* by Charlotte Unwin
- crayons, markers, or colored pencils
- marking pen
- stapler, hole punch, and yarn or hole punch and binding rings
- *Let's Pretend* Frame Sentence (page 169)
- chart paper
- poster board

Preparation:

1. Prepare a model project to show the children.
2. Create a front and back cover for the class book, using the poster board.

Directions:

Read *Let's Pretend* to the children. Discuss the occupations in the story and the facts given about them.

Have the children brainstorm different occupations they know. Record their ideas on chart paper, leaving space to the right of each for additional writing. After listing at least one idea per child, ask the children to think of one or two facts about each occupation. Record these next to the occupations.

Give each child a frame sentence page. Have the child illustrate himself or herself engaged in one of the listed occupations. Have the child or a helper complete the frame sentence and add one or two facts about that occupation.

Bind all the pages together into a class book and share it with the class, each child reading his or her own page. Add the book to the classroom library.

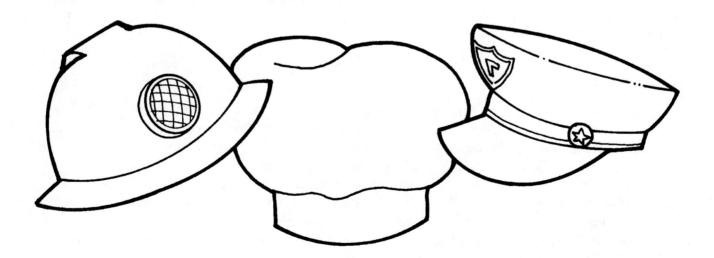

Expository Writing

Let's Pretend
(First and Second Grades)

Activity:

Each student will write a booklet about occupations.

Materials:

- *Let's Pretend* by Charlotte Unwin
- construction paper
- stapler
- pencils
- marking pen

- *Let's Pretend* Frame Sentence (page 169)
- scissors
- crayons, markers, or colored pencils
- chart paper

Preparation:

1. Prepare a model project to show the children.

2. Make a booklet for each student. To do so, staple five *Let's Pretend* Frame Sentence pages together with construction-paper covers.

Directions:

Read *Let's Pretend* to the children. Discuss the occupations in the story and the facts given about them.

Have the children brainstorm different occupations they know. Record their ideas on chart paper, leaving space to the right of each for additional writing. After listing at least one idea per child, ask the children to think of one or two facts about each occupation. Record these next to the occupations.

Give each student a booklet. Ask each one to select five occupations and to complete a page in the booklet for each occupation. On the *Let's Pretend* Frame Sentence page, the child should complete the frame sentence and write two sentences about the occupation. He or she should also color a picture of himself or herself doing the job. On the cover, each student should write a title and his or her name.

Share the completed books.

(Third Grade)

To increase the activity to third-grade (or advanced second-grade) level, forgo the reading of *Let's Pretend*. Have the students brainstorm a list of occupations they know. Record their ideas on chart paper. As a class or in small groups, write down two facts about each occupation, just enough to get their ideas flowing. Then ask each student to choose five of the occupations and require a full paragraph of five or more sentences to be written about each one. Also, older children may not be interested in imagining themselves doing the jobs, so suggest they complete illustrations of adults in the various occupations. You may even require research so that there will be authenticity to any uniforms drawn (such as a fire fighter's or police officer's). Provide the students with the sentence frame on page 169, deleting the title and the introductory words before you duplicate the sheet for them.

Expository Writing

Let's Pretend Frame Sentence

Let's pretend I am a (an) _____ .

_____

_____

_____

_____

_____

_____

_____

Expository Writing

Sentence Strip Books

Activity:

The class or individual students will create a sentence-strip book of information learned during a unit of study.

Materials:

- sentence strips
- chart paper
- pocket chart
- pencils or markers
- colored sentence strips
- marking pen
- stapler

What We Learned About Frogs
by Room 28

Preparation:

1. For kindergarten, create a front cover for a class book from a colored sentence strip.

2. For first, second, or third grades, make one book per student. To do so, bind five plain sentence strips with a colored strip for the cover. (You may wish to increase the number of pages for third graders.)

Directions:

Near or at the end of a unit of study, have the children brainstorm a list of the things they learned from the unit. Then do one of the following activities, depending on your students' grade level.

Kindergarten

Record each response on a sentence strip. Place each sentence strip in a pocket chart as completed. Have the children organize the strips. Add the colored sentence strip cover and bind the strips into a class book. Write a title and your room number (or each student's name) on the cover. Share the class book and add it to the classroom library.

First and Second Grades

Record each response on chart paper. Give each student a sentence strip booklet. Instruct each student to write one fact per page in the booklet. A title and the author's name should be written on the cover. When they are complete, have the students share their books.

Third Grade

After completing an oral brainstorming session as a class, provide each student with a booklet. Ask each student to write a fact from those they heard or others they know on each of the sentence-strip pages. A title and the author's name should be written on the cover. When complete, share the books in small groups or as a class.

Expository Writing

Let's Do It: Kindergarten

Activity:

Students will write a class book, telling the steps in completing an art project.

Materials:

- large art project
- sentence strips
- marking pen
- pocket chart

Preparation:

1. Guide each student in creating an art project with a number of steps. The project should be the same for all of them. While they work, construct the project yourself, but make yours much larger than the others. On your project, include a large display area for the class book.

2. Cut the sentence strips to fit the display area.

3. Write the title of the art project on one sentence strip and place it at the top of the pocket chart.

Directions:

After the children have completed the selected art project, have them brainstorm the steps in making the project. Encourage them to give the steps in the order that they were done. Record the students' responses on separate sentence strips and place them in the pocket chart. When the project is complete, choral read the sentences, changing the order, if necessary. Let the students direct you. Do one of two things with the sentence strips: (1) Staple them into a book and glue the back page of the book to the display area of the art project, or (2) Glue the sentence strips in order to the display area of the art project. Display the project as an example of expository writing.

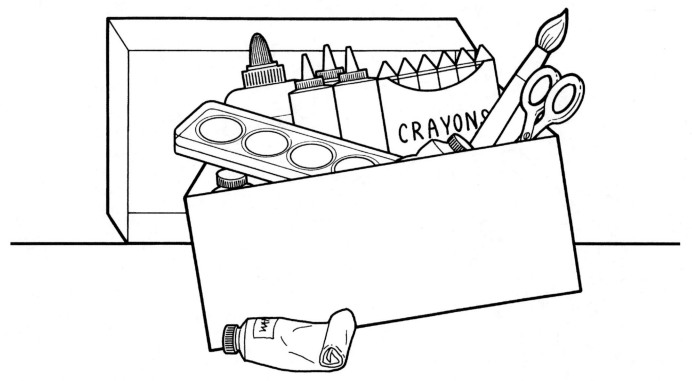

Expository Writing

Let's Do It: First, Second, and Third Grades

Activity:

Each student will write the steps in completing an art project.

Materials:

- art project (1 per student)
- pencils and paper
- Expository Writing Web 2 (page 178, 1 per student)
- Sample Expository Writing Web 2 (page 179, 1 per student)

Preparation:

Guide each student in creating an art project with a number of steps. The project should be the same for all of them. (A sample art project is illustrated below. See page 179 for a sample writing web to use as a model with this art project.)

Directions:

After the children have completed the selected art project, have them brainstorm the steps in making the project. Encourage them to give the steps in the order they were done. As they list the steps, each student should write them on the Expository Writing Web 2.

When they have completed the web, ask each student to share it with a partner, revising and editing it, as necessary. Then have the students transfer the information from the writing web to the writing paper in sentence form.

After completing their writing, instruct the students to share with a partner once more, revising and editing as necessary. A final copy of the writing should be made and attached to the art project. Allow the students to share and display their work.

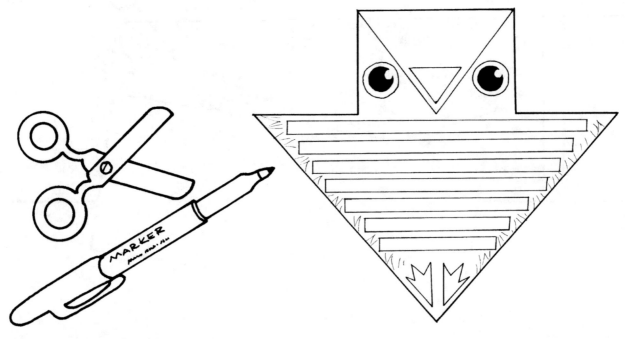

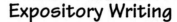

Expository Writing

Shapes, Shapes, Shapes: Kindergarten

Activity :

Students will create a class shape book about a topic of study.

Materials:

- Idea Graph for Beginning Writers (page 180)
- paper
- scissors
- chart paper
- shape template
- construction paper
- books related to selected topic
- marking pen

Preparation:

1. Choose a writing topic.

2. Select several books related to the topic the children will be writing about.

3. Create a template in a corresponding shape. For example, if you are studying frogs, make a frog template.

4. Cut the students' writing paper in the selected shape.

5. Cut front and back construction-paper covers in the same shape.

Directions:

Read to the students the books you selected. This can be done over a period of days. Afterwards, have the students brainstorm the things they have learned about the topic. They can work in small groups to make notes on the idea graph sheet. (If they are emerging writers, have an aide help them.)

Gather again as a class. Have the children share their ideas. Record their responses on chart paper in complete sentences. Choral read the responses when they are complete.

Give each student a piece of the shape paper to illustrate one of the sentences from the chart paper. The student can then copy the sentence that tells about his picture, or a helper can write the sentence for him or her. Use the covers previously created and bind the class book. Share the book and add it to the classroom library.

Expository Writing

Shapes, Shapes, Shapes: First, Second, and Third Grades

Activity:

Each students will write a shape book about a topic of study.

Materials:

- Expository Writing Notes (page 175)
- shape template
- construction paper
- pencils
- stapler

- Expository Writing Web 1 (page 176)
- writing paper
- scissors
- books related to selected topic

Preparation:

Prepare a shape template for each student's topic of choice. If you are studying lions, for example, make a lions template. If desired, have the students work on the same topic so that you need make only one shape. (You can allow older students to make their own templates.)

Directions:

Over a period of days, have the students read books on a topic of your/their choice. While reading, the children should record things they learn about the topic. They can take notes on the Expository Writing Notes sheet. Using the Expository Writing Notes sheet, the students can then fill in the Expository Writing Web 1. The information on the Expository Writing Web 1 is then used to write an expository piece. (A sample web is provided on page 177. You may wish to use it as a model before students complete page 176.) Provide each student with writing paper, two sheets of construction paper, a shape template, a pencil, and scissors. Have them make two shape covers and as many shape writing sheets as needed. The students can write their expository piece on the shape writing paper and a title and author's name on the front cover. Staple the sheets together to make a book. Have the students share their books with the class.

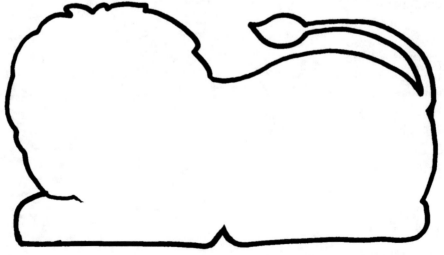

Expository Writing

Expository Writing Notes

Name: _____

Title or Topic:

Step or Idea: _____

_____

Details:

Step or Idea: _____

_____

Details:

Step or Idea: _____

_____

Details:

Step or Idea: _____

_____

Details:

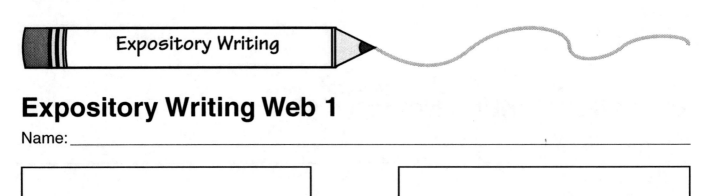

Expository Writing

Expository Writing Web 1

Name: _____

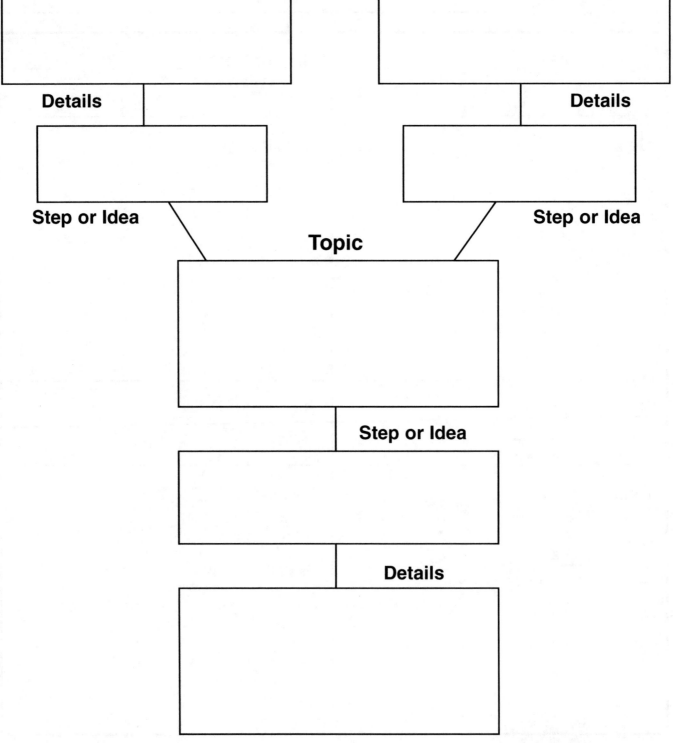

Details

Step or Idea

Details

Step or Idea

Topic

Step or Idea

Details

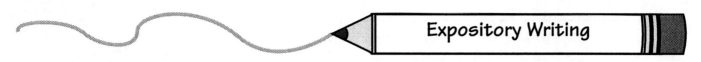

Expository Writing

Sample Expository Writing Web 1

Name: _____

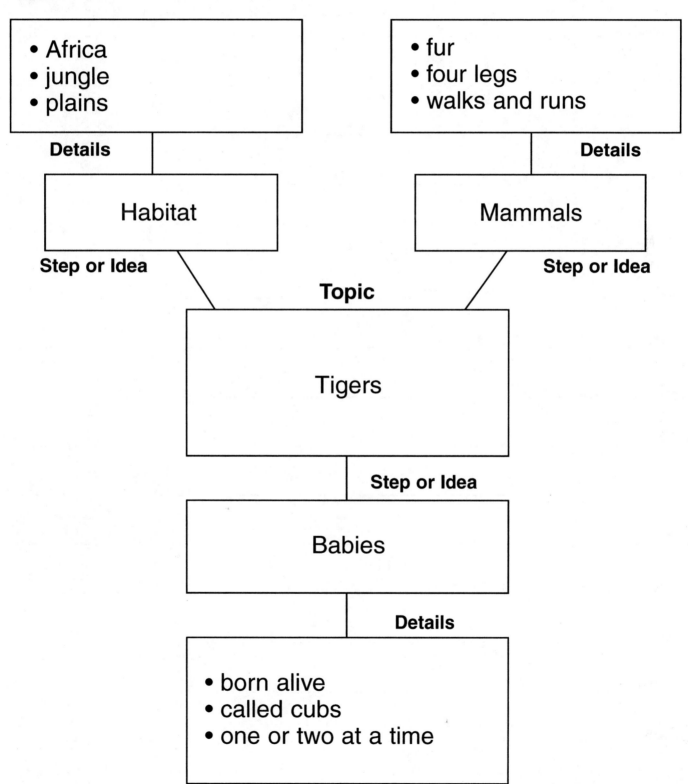

- Africa
- jungle
- plains

Details

Habitat

Step or Idea

- fur
- four legs
- walks and runs

Details

Mammals

Step or Idea

Topic

Tigers

Step or Idea

Babies

Details

- born alive
- called cubs
- one or two at a time

Expository Writing

Expository Writing Web 2

Name:_____

Title: _____

Materials needed: _____   _____

                            _____   _____

                            _____   _____

1st_____

2nd _____

3rd _____

4th_____

5th_____

6th_____

7th_____

8th_____

9th_____

10th_____

Last_____

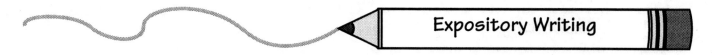

Sample Expository Writing Web 2

Name: _____

Title: Hooty Owl

Materials Needed:

brown construction paper	orange construction paper
scissors	white construction paper
black construction paper	glue

1st Fold the brown paper square on the diagonal to form a triangle.

2nd Open the brown paper square and fold on the other diagonal to form a triangle.

3rd Open the brown paper and fold down the top corner to the middle to form part of the owl's head.

4th To finish the head, cut straight down from one of the top points to the fold and then along the center fold toward the outer edge. Do the same on the other side, starting at the other top point.

5th Fringe the edges of the bottom triangle to make it look like the feathers of an owl's body.

6th Cut two large circles from the white paper and glue them on the owl's head for the whites of its eyes.

7th Cut two large circles from the black paper (smaller than the white circles) and glue them on top of the white circles to make the owl's eyes.

Last Cut two feet and a triangle beak from the orange paper and glue them to the owl to complete it.

Expository Writing

Idea Graph for Beginning Writers

(Expository Writing Notes)

Name: _____

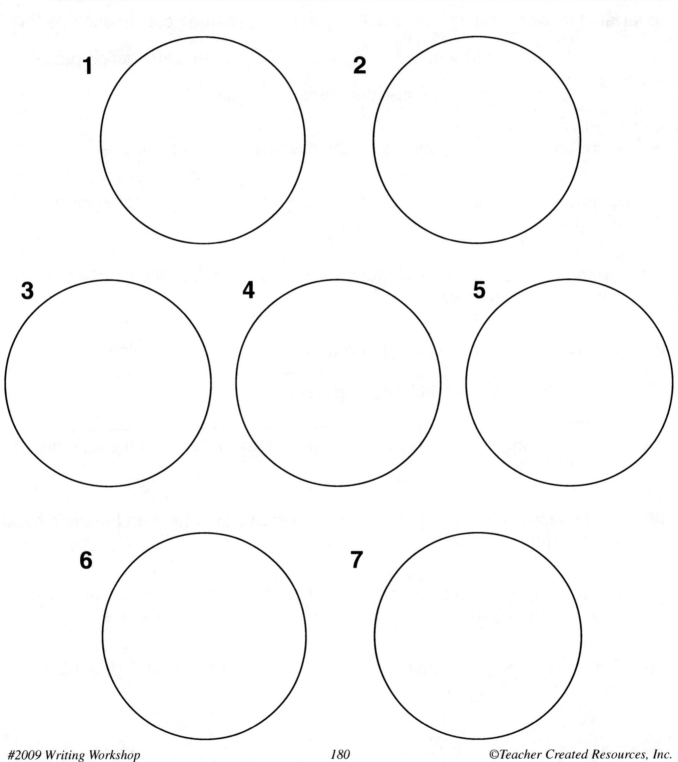

Sample Expository Writing Frame Sentences

Topic: Animals

- This animal eats _____.
- The color of this animal is _____.
- This animal's body is covered with _____.
- This animal moves by _____.
- This animal's babies are called _____.
- This animal lives in _____.

Topic: Biographies

- _____ was born on _____.
- _____ lived in _____.
- _____ was famous because _____.

Topic: Space

- This planet is _____ miles from the sun.
- This planet is the _____ planet from the sun.
- The color of this planet is _____.
- The temperature on this planet is _____.

Topic: Dinosaurs

- This dinosaur lived during the _____ period.
- This dinosaur was as big as _____.
- This dinosaur had _____teeth and ate _____.
- This dinosaur walked on _____ feet.
- This dinosaur's nickname is _____.

Topic: China

- China is about the same size as _____.
- _____ people live in China today.
- The major crops in China are _____.
- The major industries in China are _____.

Topic: Self

- I am _____ years old.
- I live in the city of _____.
- My hair is _____.
- My eyes are _____.
- My favorite thing to do is _____.

Organizing for Writing

Preparing Notebooks and Folders

Materials:

- 1 spiral-bound composition notebook per student
- 1 pocket folder per student
- containers to hold several folders
- marker

Directions:

1. Divide the students into groups according to the number of folders each container will hold. It is very helpful if each group has a differently colored writing folder.

2. Label each folder "Writing Folder" and each notebook "Writing Notebook." Also label each folder and notebook with its owner's name.

3. Label each container with the names of the students whose writing folders it contains.

4. Place the writing folders in the containers in your classroom writing center.

5. Have the students write the first draft of their stories in their writing notebooks. Instruct the students to write on only one side of the paper. (The other side can be used to insert new ideas when revising the story, using asterisks to mark insertions.)

6. Each time you begin your writing workshop session, select one child from each group to pass out the writing folders. The same child will be responsible for collecting the writing folders at the conclusion of the writing workshop session.

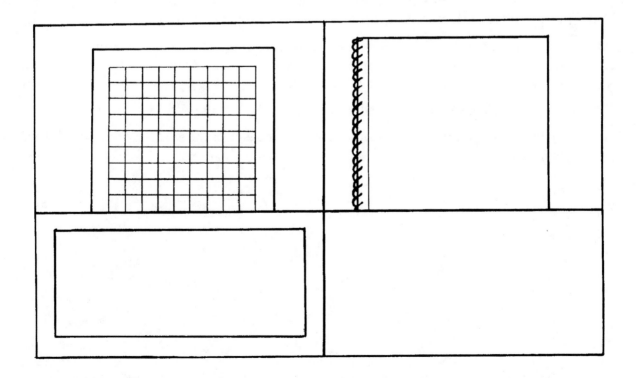

Organizing Student Materials

Writing Folder Contents

Materials:

- Writing Notebooks
- Important Words List (page 185)
- Writing Workshop Daily Record (page 188)
- Writing Folders
- Transition Words lists (pages 186 and 187)
- stories in the publishing process

Directions:

1. Make one copy of the Important Words List for each student. Attach the list to the outside of one pocket inside each Writing Folder. Also store a Transition Words list inside each Writing Folder.

2. Make one copy of the Writing Workshop Daily Record for each student. Attach the record to the inside of each Writing Folder.

3. Make extra copies of the Writing Workshop Daily Record on page 188 and place them in a box with your other writing workshop supplies.

4. Those children whose writing demands correct spelling can use the Important Words List while writing. It is useful for those students who become so involved in their writing content that they do not wish to bother looking up the words. These students become much better at using developmental spelling, which actually advances them to conventional spelling much more quickly.

5. The Transition Words pages will help students in all sorts of writing. Be sure they keep it handy, and remind them often of its existence so that they remember to utilize it. (Feel free to add words to the Important Words List as needed.)

6. At the conclusion of each writing workshop session, instruct the students to complete their daily record by writing the date and checking all appropriate boxes. When a new sheet is needed, a student can staple it over the completed sheet.

7. The Writing Notebook should be stored in the right pocket of the Writing Folder.

8. Stories that are being illustrated are stored in the left pocket of the Writing Folder. (This keeps the edges neat.)

Important Words List

A	**D**	**H**	**O**	**T**	**W**
about	done	help	of	the	was
again	does	here	once	there	went
always	**E**	have	out	them	were
another	enough	**L**	**P**	they	what
are	ever	like	people	this	where
around	every	look	play	to	who
away	**F**	**M**	**R**	together	why
B	few	many	right	**U**	work
because	for	**N**	**S**	until	would
brother	found	never	said	**V**	**Y**
C	from	next	saw	very	you
children	friend	night	sister		your
come	**G**		some		
	good		something		

Additional Words

_____   _____   _____

_____   _____   _____

_____   _____   _____

Organizing Student Materials

Transition Words

Size Transitions

the largest	equal to	the small-sized	the shortest	the tallest
the next largest	smaller than	the medium-sized	larger than	
the smallest	the smallest	the large-sized	the next smallest	

Time Transitions

then	finally	before noon	today	immediately
next	the next day	in the afternoon	tomorrow	before
at last	in the next few years	in the evening	in the future	during
now		two weeks later	the most recent	after
soon	at the beginning	thereafter	the day after tomorrow	this year
then	in the middle	presently		the earliest
later	at the end	soon thereafter	the first	in the past
first	after a short time	by this time	a more recent	next year
second	simultaneously	afterwards	the next earliest	
third	in the morning	yesterday	six months later	

Space Transitions

behind	throughout	inside	at the end of	high
over	south of	next to	between	against
under	close to	down	on the edge of	alongside
below	on top of	up	east of	inside
beneath	at the top	west of	north of	here
low down	by	facing	side by side	there
in	in front of	in back of	in the center of	beyond
on	around	to the right of	on the bottom	farther on
beside	near	to the left of	on the corner	
toward	ahead of	outside	above	

Transition Words *(cont.)*

Importance Transitions

the best	the most important	more important than	the next best
the next best	equally important	most important	the worst
the least best	the next important	the best	
the least important	the first		

Chain-Link Transitions

one example of	in the first place	for instance	the third	one
on the other hand	in the second place	also	besides	as
another example		moreover	a further	similarly
a further example	in the third place	another	still	while
still another	for example	further	likewise	although
in addition	in the same way	lastly	last	first
to the contrary	consequently	the last	even if	second
on the contrary	in contrast	nonetheless	instead	third
despite the	in spite of	indeed	after all	
even though	nevertheless	naturally	the first	
more specifically	specifically	on the one hand	the second	
similar to is	in other words	in fact	again	

Concluding Transitions

to conclude	therefore	in short	thus	finally
in conclusion	in sum	to sum up	as you can see	
in summary	in brief	to summarize	as a result	

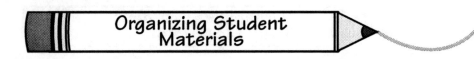

Organizing Student
Materials

Writing Workshop Daily Record

Name:_____

Today I . . .

Date								
worked on writing a story.								
read my story to myself.								
had a peer conference.								
revised my story.								
edited my story.								
had a teacher conference.								
illustrated my story.								

V.I.B.s (Very Important Books)

Being completely prepared before you begin your writing workshop will help you to have confidence while encouraging your students to reach their full potentials as writers in your classroom. Following is a complete organizational plan for taking student writing through to its publication as a V.I.B. (Very Important Book).

Materials:

- 6–8 red pens
- I Need a Conference sign-up sheet (page 191)
- 4 plastic, stacking paper trays
- title page borders (pages 192–201)
- hanging file folder container
- Story Reflections (page 203)
- laminating machine
- spiral binding machine
- V.I.B. Label (page 205)

- red pen container
- computer and printer
- construction paper
- hanging file folders
- Publishing Checklists (page 202)
- Parent Instruction Letter (page 204)
- spiral binders
- large brown envelopes

Directions:

1. **Red Pens:** Put the red pens in a container and place them next to the Writing Folders. The children use these for editing. Students are often motivated to proofread when they can use the red pen to add missing capital letters and periods.

2. **Conferences:** Hang the I Need a Conference sign-up sheet (page 191) in a location convenient for both the students and the teacher. Students should work on another story while waiting for a conference. (The teacher must conduct student conferences every spare minute she or he can, because there will be a backup of students waiting once your writing workshop is under way.)

3. **Typed Stories:** Obtain a parent volunteer to type the children's stories or type them yourself on the computer. In the primary grades, the writing process is what is important. Therefore, it is expeditious to have an adult type the children's stories. However, if handwriting practice is the goal, the children can certainly recopy their stories by hand. (However, be prepared for them to make different mistakes and to become disinterested in writing stories of any quality.)

   It is suggested that you type most stories in three pages, one for the beginning, one for the middle, and one for the end. Each story should also have a typed title page containing the title of the story, the author's name, and the date of publication. Typed stories are placed inside the child's writing notebook and then placed on one of the plastic stacking trays. These writing notebooks and typed stories are distributed to the students during the next writing workshop session.

Publishing Stories

V.I.B.s (Very Important Books) *(cont.)*

4. **Story Covers:** Cut construction paper for story covers and store them on a stacking tray in the writing center. The children should use two pieces of the same color of paper for their covers. Only the front needs to be illustrated.

5. **Title Pages:** Make several copies of the title pages from which the students can choose. Store each in a different hanging file folder in the folder container and place them in the writing center.

6. **Publishing Checklists:** Photocopy several copies of the Publishing Checklists and put them in the writing center. These are to be filled out for each story as the child checks to be sure he or she has done everything necessary to have a story published.

7. **Completed Stories:** Provide a place for the children to put stories that are ready for the editor's examination. Use a plastic stacking tray in the writing center.

8. **Story Reflections:** Photocopy the Story Reflections sheet (page 203) and the Parent Instruction Letter (page 204). The Story Reflections sheet is bound at the end of every story. The Parent Instruction Letter is slipped inside the front cover of the story before the child takes it home to share the story with his or her parents.

9. **Story Binding:** After a story has passed the editor's inspection, laminate the covers and bind the book, using a spiral binding machine. There are many other ways to publish children's stories. However, this is usually the most professional looking way, and it adds to the value placed on the stories. Initially, each story is bound individually. At the end of the year, each student's stories can be bound into an anthology. The students can illustrate a special cover for their anthologies.

10. **V.I.B. Envelopes:** Make five copies of the V.I.B. Label and attach each to a large, brown envelope. Laminate the envelopes for durability since they will be used often. After an author has shared his or her published story with the class, slip the story inside a V.I.B. envelope and send it home to be shared with the author's family. All stories are to be returned the next day. They should become part of the classroom library until the end of the year when they are bound into an anthology and sent home to be cherished forever.

I Need a Conference

Sign your name on the list when you are ready for a teacher-student writing conference.

	Name		Name
1		11	
2		12	
3		13	
4		14	
5		15	
6		16	
7		17	
8		18	
9		19	
10		20	

Publishing Stories

Title Page 1

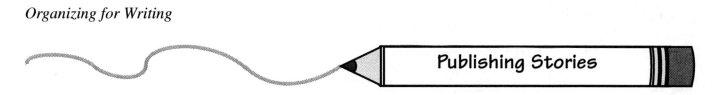

Title Page 2

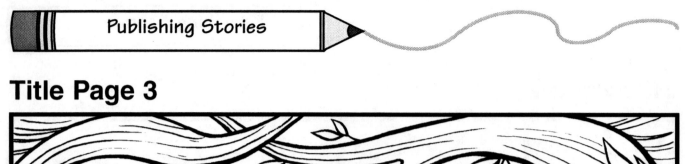

Publishing Stories

Title Page 3

Title Page 4

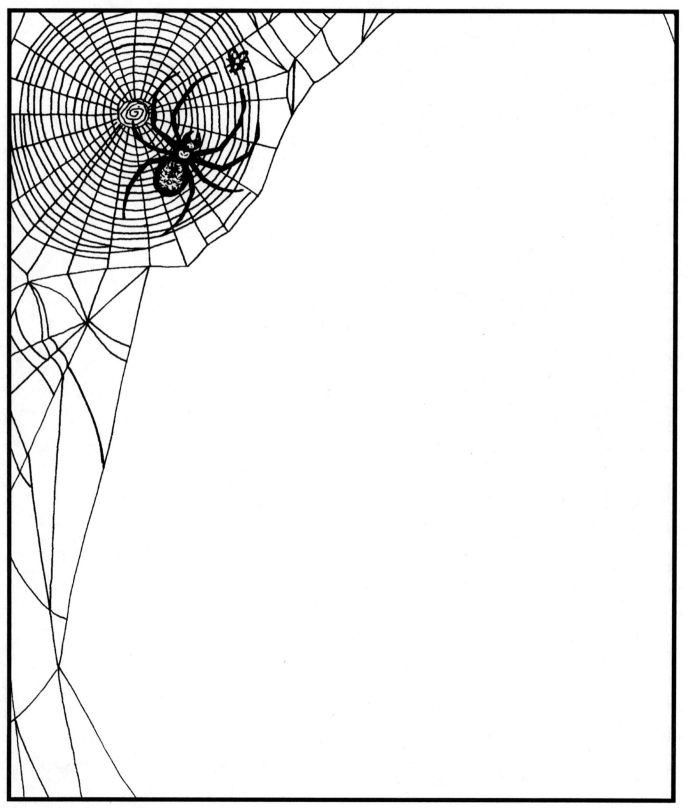

Publishing Stories

Title Page 5

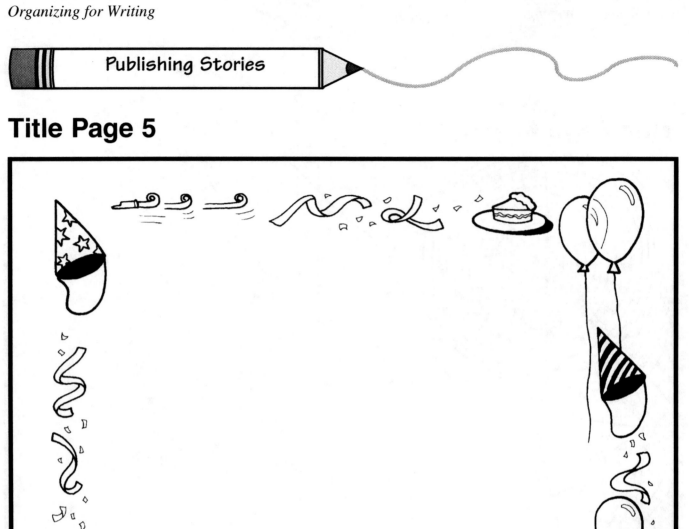

Title Page 6

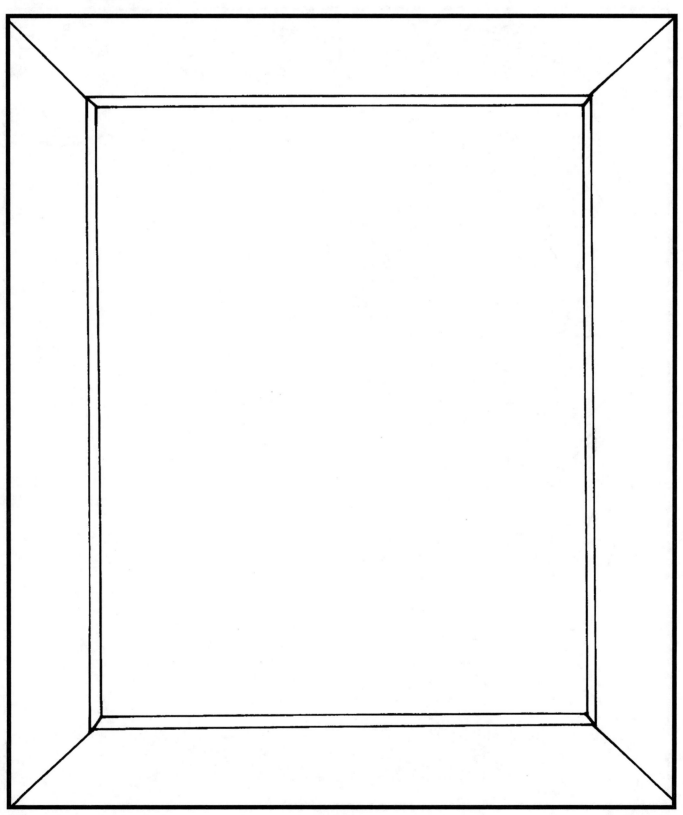

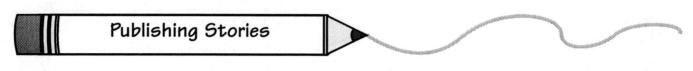

Publishing Stories

Title Page 7

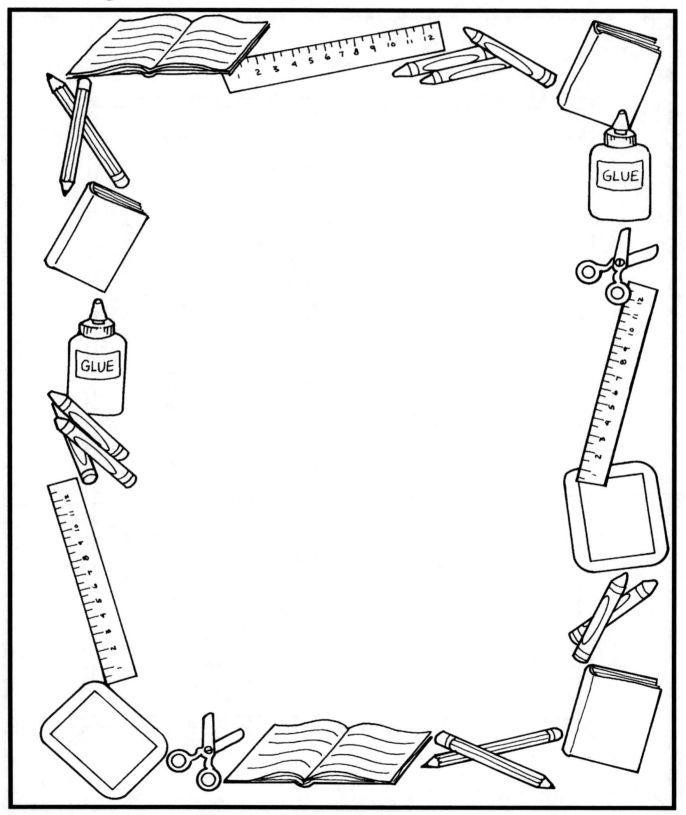

Publishing Stories

Title Page 8

Publishing Stories

Title Page 9

Title Page 10

Publishing Stories

Publishing Checklists

Name:_____

Date:_____

Here is your publishing checklist. Check (✔) each item as you complete it.

Cover

- ☐ title
- ☐ author's name
- ☐ whole picture

Title Page

- ☐ title
- ☐ author's name
- ☐ whole picture

Story

- ☐ all pictures complete
- ☐ revised and edited
- ☐ neat copy ready

Name:_____

Date:_____

Here is your publishing checklist. Check (✔) each item as you complete it.

Cover

- ☐ title
- ☐ author's name
- ☐ whole picture

Title Page

- ☐ title
- ☐ author's name
- ☐ whole picture

Story

- ☐ all pictures complete
- ☐ revised and edited
- ☐ neat copy ready

Publishing Stories

Story Reflections

Name:_____ Date: _____

Title of Story _____

Grade _____   Teacher _____

I think this story shows that I can...

_____

_____

_____

My parent(s) think this story shows that I can...

_____

_____

_____

My teacher thinks this story shows that I can...

_____

_____

_____

Publishing Stories

Parent Instruction Letter

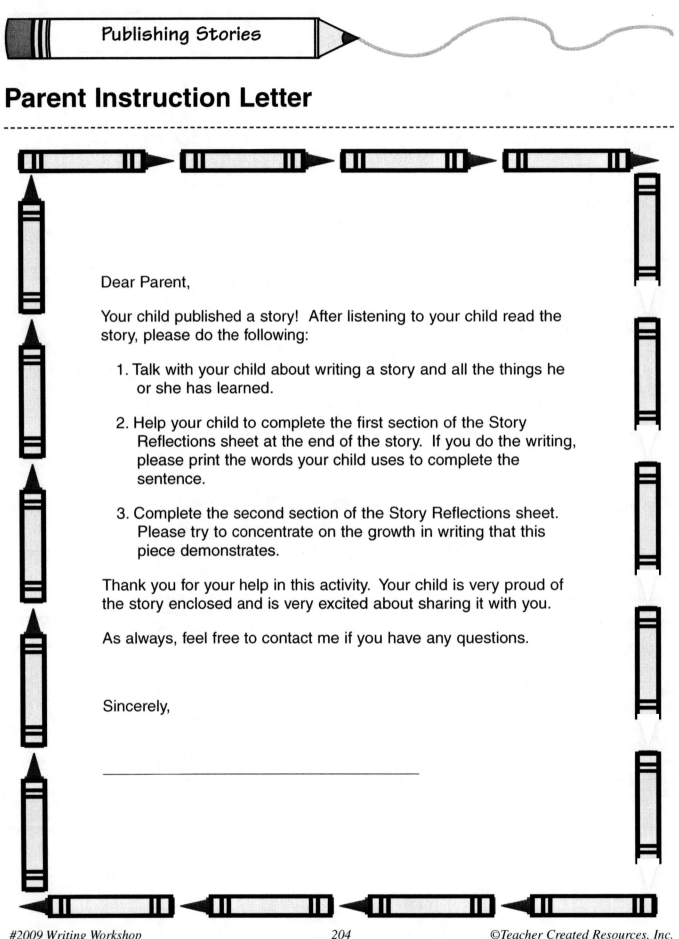

Dear Parent,

Your child published a story! After listening to your child read the story, please do the following:

1. Talk with your child about writing a story and all the things he or she has learned.

2. Help your child to complete the first section of the Story Reflections sheet at the end of the story. If you do the writing, please print the words your child uses to complete the sentence.

3. Complete the second section of the Story Reflections sheet. Please try to concentrate on the growth in writing that this piece demonstrates.

Thank you for your help in this activity. Your child is very proud of the story enclosed and is very excited about sharing it with you.

As always, feel free to contact me if you have any questions.

Sincerely,

_____

V.I.B. Label

Inside you will find a

Your child has published a book! Please read it together tonight. Be sure your child brings it back to school tomorrow. The rest of the class is waiting to read the story, too. Your child's published stories will be kept at school until the end of the year. At that time, they will be bound into an anthology and brought home.

*Very Important Book

_____   _____
School Name   Room Number

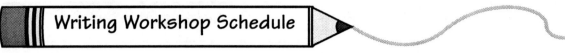

Writing Workshop Schedule

There are many ways to structure your writing workshop time. The goal is to have the children take as much of the responsibility as possible for the writing workshop and to encourage their interest and enthusiasm in writing.

Allow between thirty to ninety minutes four times a week for structured writing workshop. Begin writing workshop in January in first grade and allow approximately thirty minutes during the beginning weeks. As the children become more involved in writing and there are stories to edit and share, much more time is required. Second and third grade teachers should begin writing workshop at the beginning of the school year, and they should begin with forty-five minute sessions four or five times a week.

There are many different stages to writing a story which allow the children to participate in several different activities during a writing workshop session. During April and May, the ninety minutes will seem to fly by as the children work hard to publish their stories. Those children who find a real interest in writing are encouraged to work on their stories during any free-choice time you might have during your day.

Lesson Plan for Writing Workshop

Following is a plan for a standard writing workshop session:

The teacher says, "Boys and girls, it is writing workshop time. Please join me on the rug." The children sit on the rug in their assigned spots. "We have some stories to edit today." The teacher holds up the cover, title page, and story pages and runs through the Publishing Checklist form. It is the children's responsibility to approve for publication or reject as an unfinished story. They indicate by using the silent signal (thumbs-up or thumbs-down) as the teacher reads each item on the checklist. If a page receives thumbs-down, call on a child (not the author) to tell what is missing so the author knows what to do to receive a thumbs-up the next time. Using the author's classmates as editors eliminates rejection by the teacher of the child's efforts.

"We have some published stories to share today," adds the teacher. The teacher holds up the first story to be shared, and the author comes forward and sits in the special "author's chair" to read the story.

Organizing for Writing

Publishing Stories

Publishing Checklists

Name:_____
Date:_____
Here is your publishing checklist Check (✔) each item as you complete

Cover
☐ title
☐ author's name
☐ whole picture

Title Page
☐ title
☐ author's name
☐ whole picture

Story
☐ all pictures complete
☐ revised and edited
☐ neat copy ready

Name:_____
Date:_____
Here is your publishing checklist Check (✔) each item as you complete

Cover
☐ title
☐ author's name
☐ whole picture

Title Page
☐ title
☐ author's name
☐ whole picture

Story
☐ all pictures complete
☐ revised and edited
☐ neat copy ready

#2009 Writing Workshop

©Teacher Created Materials, Inc.

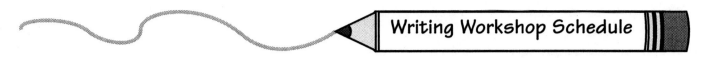

Writing Workshop Schedule

When the story sharing time is complete, the teacher may say, "We will have five minutes of write time today. I will start the timer when everyone has his or her writing notebook open and a pencil in hand." Have selected children pass out the writing folders. Start the timer when everyone is ready.

When the timer begins, use a class list to keep track of what each child will be working on during writing workshop. Call each child's name, and as each is called, have the child respond by saying either "one" or "two." One means writing a story or any facet thereof, and two means illustrating a story for publication. Set a limit of three days for illustrations per story. After three writing workshop sessions, the child must find some other time to finish the illustrations that are not complete.

After five minutes of write time and declaring the activity for the rest of the writing workshop, the children can work independently. The teacher meets with children for writing conferences during this time.

Writing workshop concludes with the children completing the Writing Workshop Daily Record forms inside their writing folders and putting all materials away. Writing folders are collected by the same children who passed them out at the beginning of the session.

Organizing for Writing

Organizing Student Materials

Writing Workshop Daily Record

Name: _____

Today

	Date							
worked on writing a story.								
read my story to myself.								
had a peer conference.								
revised my story.								
edited my story.								
had a teacher conference.								
illustrated my story.								

Classroom Display Cards

The cards on pages 208–240 may be reproduced and displayed on classroom walls, charts, or bulletin boards. Enlarge the cards as needed. They may be used to introduce, reinforce, or review some of the important ideas and terms included in this book.

Stories have a . . .

beginning,

a middle,

and an end.

Classroom Display Cards

Noun

A noun is a word that names a person, a place, or a thing.

Verb

A verb is a word that shows action. It tells what people, places, and things do.

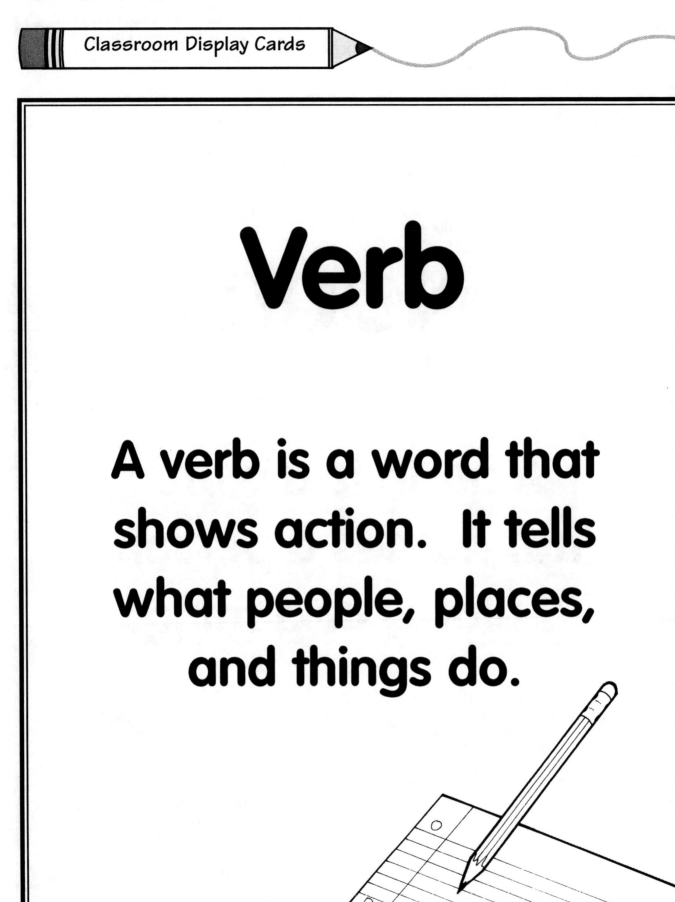

Adjective

An adjective is a word that tells about a noun. It adds detail about the noun, telling what kind, or how many. An adjective can also be used to compare nouns.

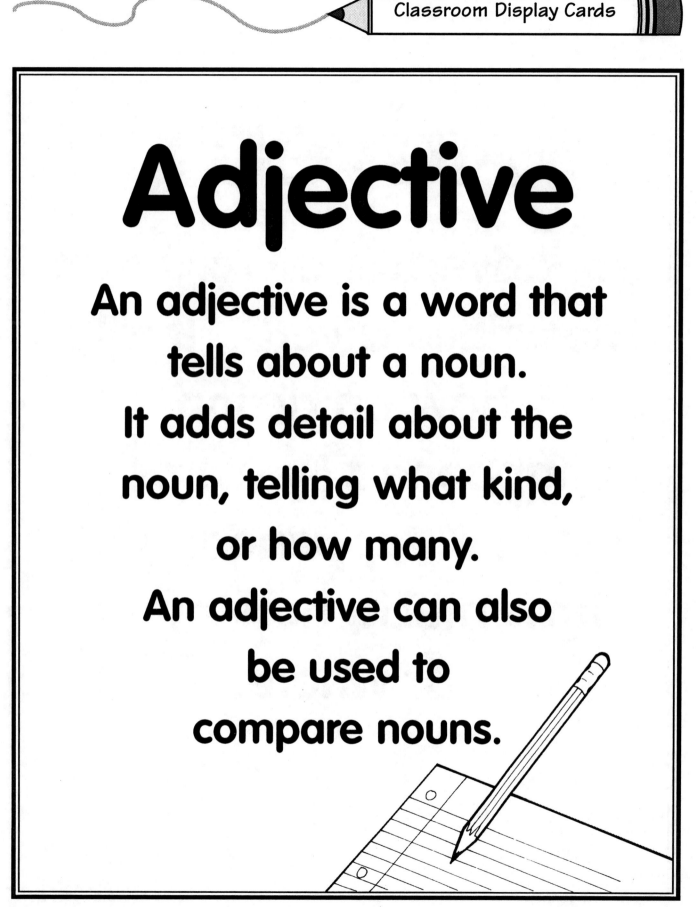

Adverb

An adverb is a word that describes a verb. It tells how an action happened (ly words), when it happened, why, how much, how often, or where.

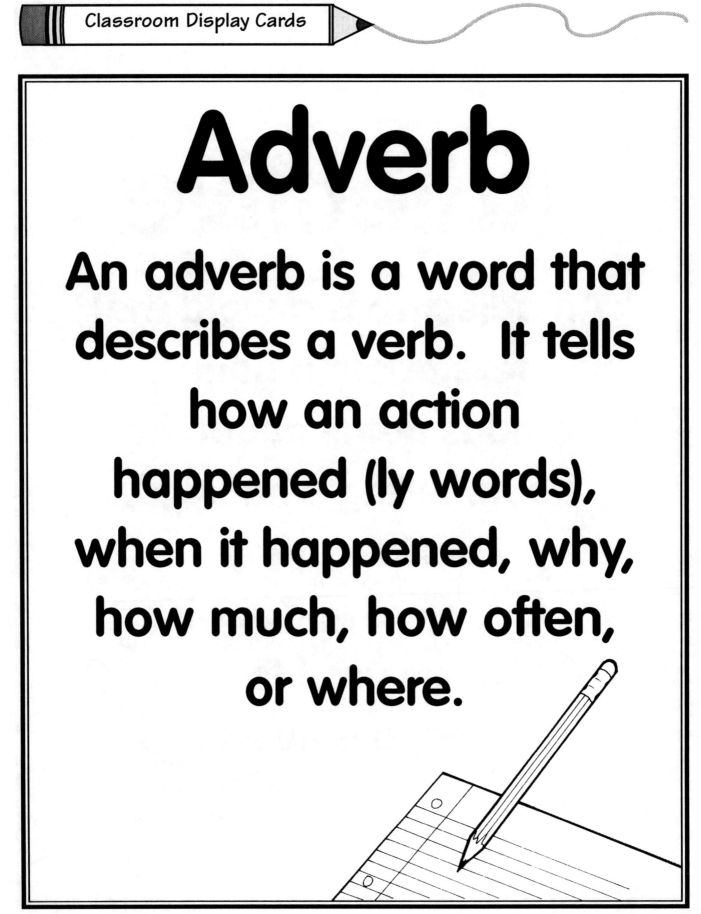

Antonym

An antonym is a word that means the opposite of another word.

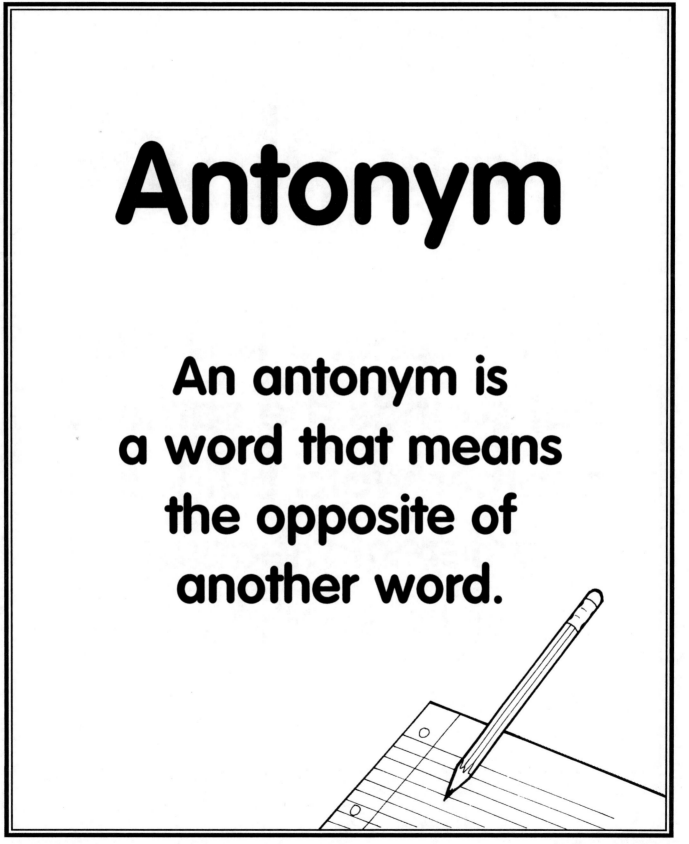

Classroom Display Cards

Homophone

A homophone is a word that sounds the same as another word but has a different meaning and spelling.

Synonym

A synonym is a word that has the same or almost the same meaning as another word.

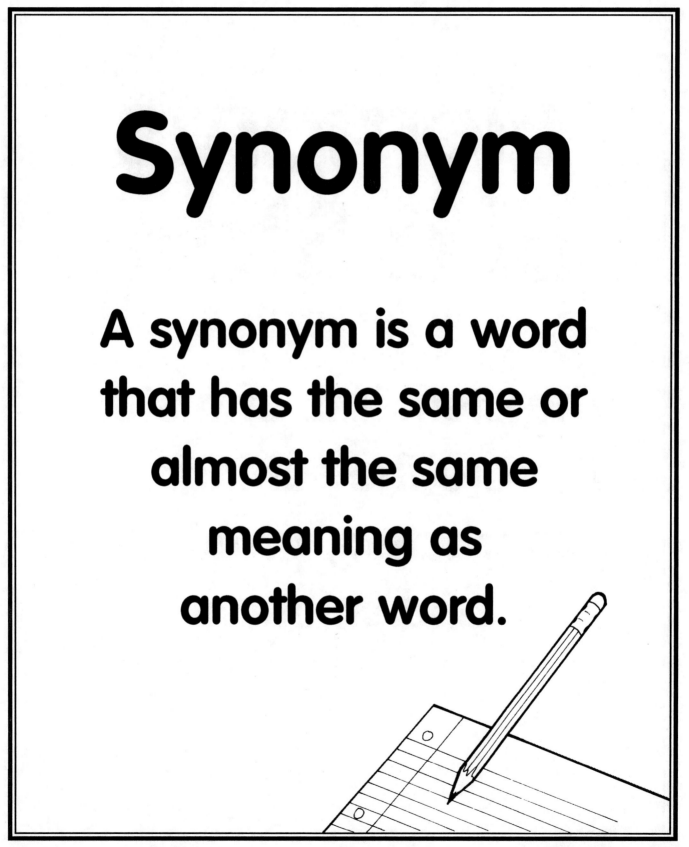

Classroom Display Cards

Elements of a Story

The elements of a story are the setting, characters, problem, and solution.

Setting

A story's setting tells where and when the story takes place.

Characters

A story's characters are the people and animals in it.

Problem

The story's problem is a conflict, disagreement, or trouble concerning one (or more) main character.

Solution

A story's solution is the answer to the problem.

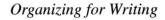

Classroom Display Cards

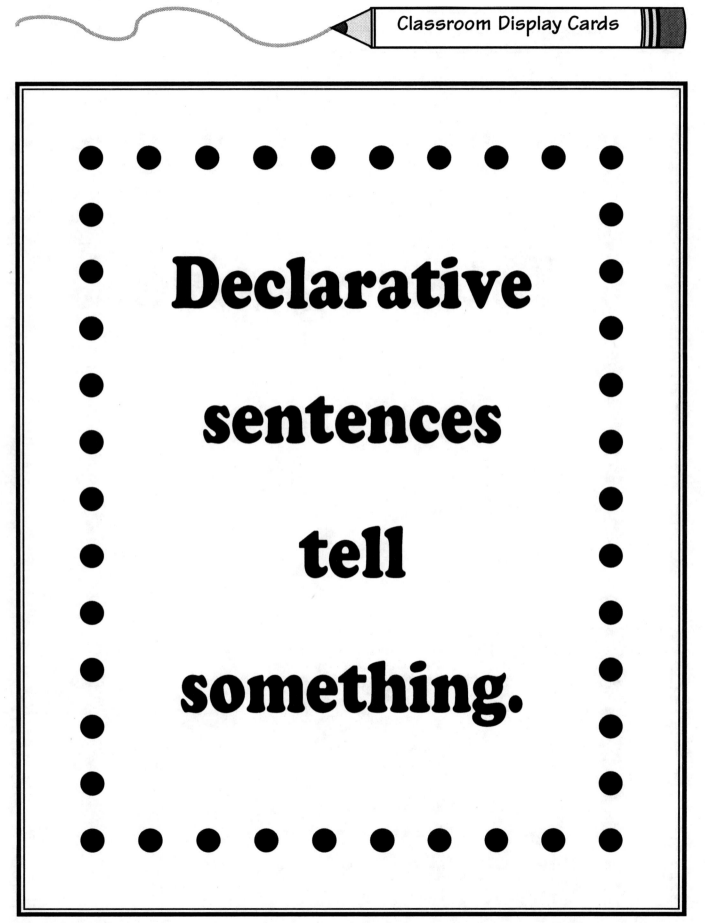

Declarative sentences tell something.

Classroom Display Cards

Interrogative sentences ask something.

220

Who or what who can stories be about?

The Circus
Clown

Classroom Display Cards

What kinds of problems can be found in stories?

Classroom Display Cards

How can

stories begin?

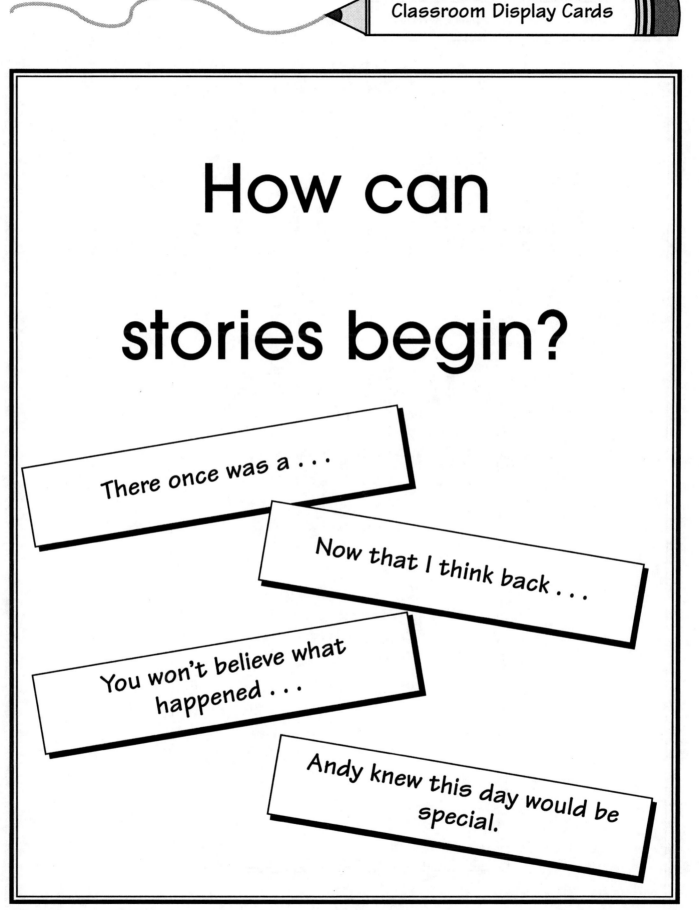

There once was a . . .

Now that I think back . . .

You won't believe what happened . . .

Andy knew this day would be special.

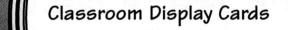

Classroom Display Cards

How to Publish

a Story

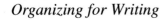

Classroom Display Cards

1.

Think of

an idea.

Classroom Display Cards

2.

Write your story.

Classroom Display Cards

3.

Read your story. Point to each word as you read it. Add any missing words, capital letters, and end punctuations.

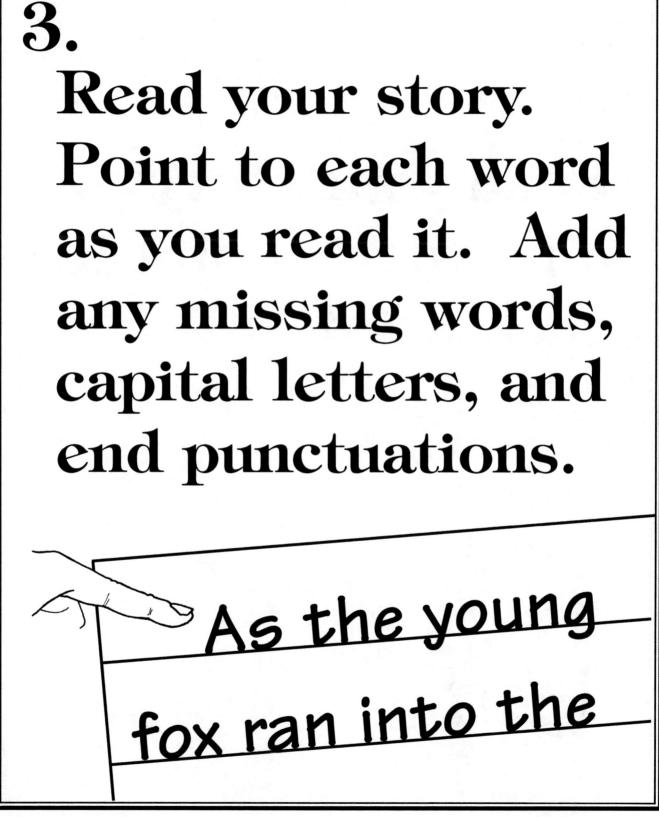

As the young

fox ran into the

4.

Read your story to a partner. Point to each word.

5.

Revise your story. Add more details to make your story better.

Classroom Display Cards

6.

Edit your story. Check for capital letters, end punctuation, check spelling.

Classroom Display Cards

7.

Sign up for a writing conference.

Conference		
Name	Time	Story

8.

Illustrate your story.

9.

Have your story bound. Display your story or add it to a portfolio or writing book.

Editing Tips

To edit your story, look carefully for ways to correct it and to make it more interesting.

- **Did you remember correct punctuation?**

- **Can you add or change parts of your story to make it say what you wanted it to say?**

- **Is it interesting to read?**

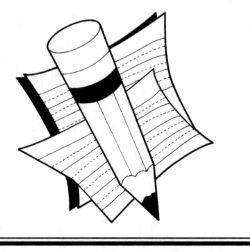

Editing Tips

To be a good peer listener, remember these tips.

1. Listen carefully to your partner's story.

2. Share with your partner positive ways to make his or her story better.

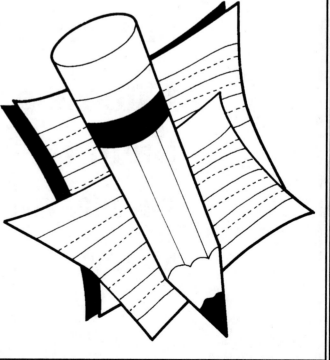

Editing Tips

To make your story better, remember these tips.

1. **Review all the ideas you received during your peer conference.**

2. **Think of some more ideas of your own.**

3. **Choose a few ideas and use them to revise your story.**

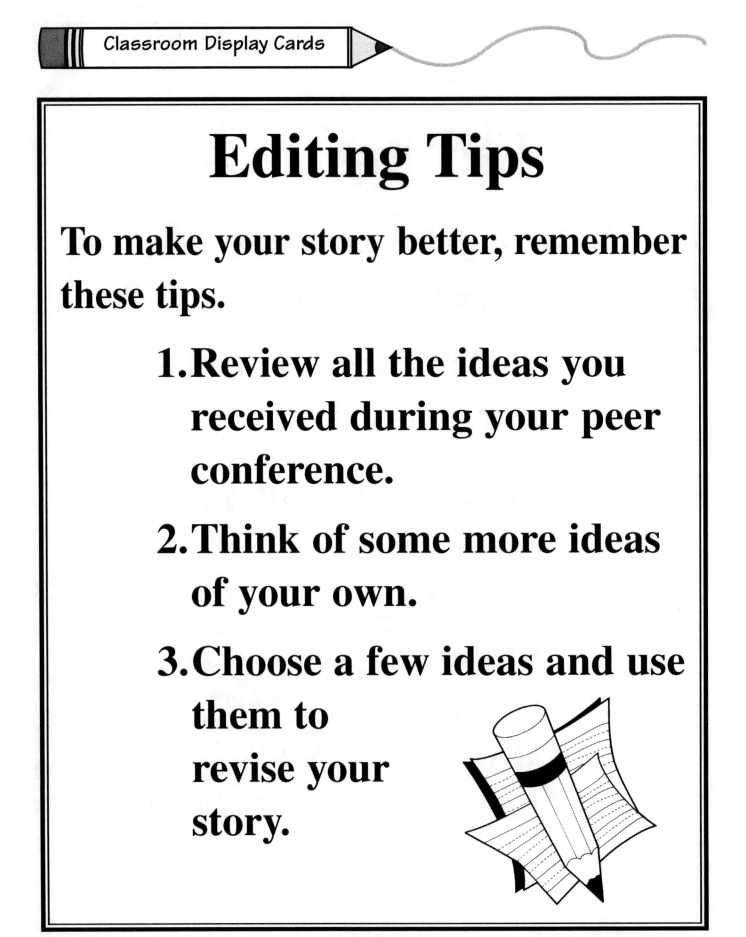

Classroom Display Cards

Narrative Writing

Telling

a Story

Classroom Display Cards

Persuasive Writing

Convincing Someone

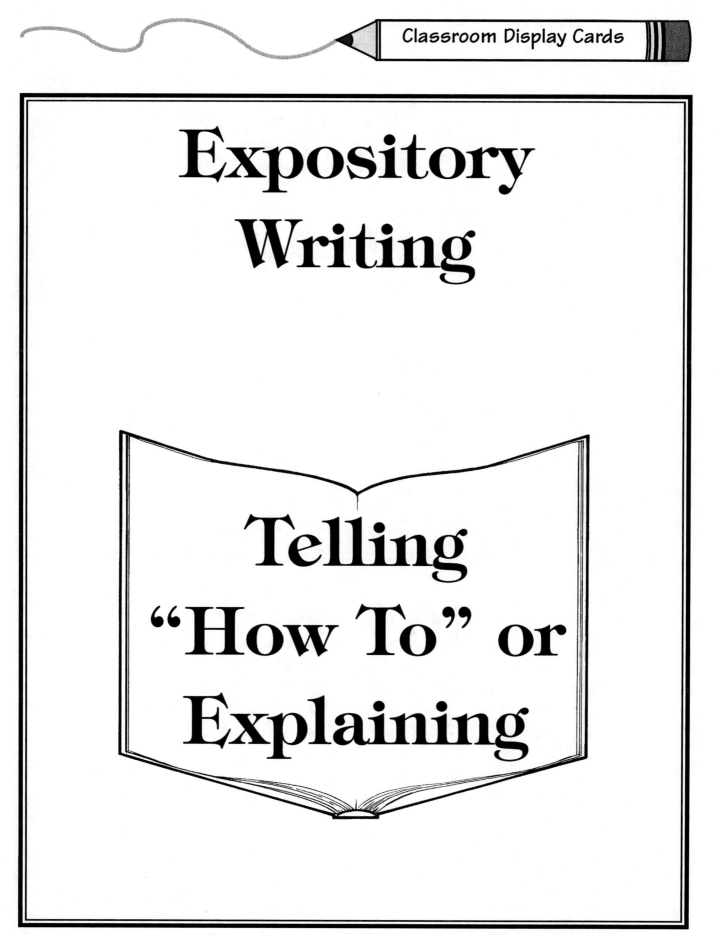

Expository Writing

Telling "How To" or Explaining

Classroom Display Cards

Letter Writing

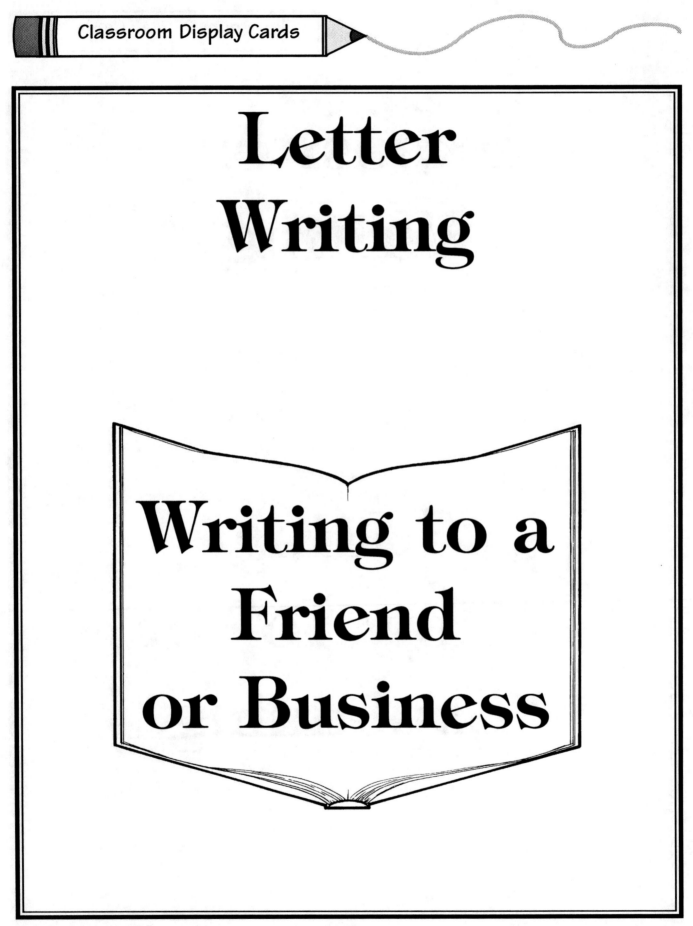

Writing to a Friend or Business

Glossary of Writing Terms

Conventions: The use of standard written English.

Edit: This term refers to the two stages in making writing correct for the reader.
- revision stage—major restructuring, reordering, and clarification of text and
- editing stage—correcting the mechanics, spelling, and punctuation

Expository: The text explains, interprets, or describes something based upon the writer's experience or research. The text differs from narrative in that the writer does not include reactions or feelings in describing or presenting information.

Focus: The clarity with which the piece presents a main idea, point of view, theme, or unifying event is the focus of the piece.

Form/Structure: This involves the construction, organization, design, and sequence of ideas in a piece of writing which make its meaning and development clear or which make it specific to the genre. It also includes the way the writing begins and the arrangement and sequencing of the material.

Genre: A literary type featuring its own group of attributes is a genre.

Integration: Integration is the manner in which the piece effectively uses the basic features to address the assignment and puts those features together to integrate the writing.

Narrative: There are two types of narrative text. In the first, the writer recounts and reflects upon a personally significant experience. In the second, the writer reports and records reactions to an observed event. The personal narrative describes both the action and the writer's reactions. A third-person narrative tells about an event and describes the reactions of the participants.

Organization: The clear, coherent, and logical flow of ideas and the explicit structure of the text makes up the organization of a piece of writing.

Persuasive: There are two types of persuasive texts. In the first, the writer takes a position and develops one side of an argument. In the second, the writer develops both a problem and a solution.

Support: The degree to which the main point or event is elaborated and explained by specific details and reasons determines its support.

Voice: The aspects of a piece of writing that give it a personal flavor and an expression of the writer's confidence are its voice.

Writing Criteria

Purpose and Meaning

- Does the writing say something?
- Does it have meaning?
- Is the purpose reflected in the form?

Authority

- Does the writing show that the author knows the topic?
- Is early interest sustained?
- Does the writing reflect personal voice?
- Is the writing honest?

Clarity

- Is the writing clear and informative?
- Is there adequate information?
- Is the information accurate?
- Is there evidence of revision?

Genre and Structure

- Does the writing have structure, order, and coherence, showing a well-developed sequence of ideas?
- Is there an effective opening, middle, and ending?
- Is there well-structured paragraphing?
- Does the writing have appropriate form?

Support

- Are all main points explained and elaborated by credible, specific details?
- Is the support balanced equally for all points discussed?

Organization

- Is the argument/plan evident?
- Are the divisions of major reasons/arguments distinct paragraphs?
- Are all points logically developed and interrelated with no digression?

Title

- Is the title appropriate?

Conventions (Spelling)

- Is the spelling accurate, or does the writing show evidence of identifying and correction of misspelled words?
- Does the writer approximate the spelling of words that are not known?

Conventions (Vocabulary)

- Is appropriate vocabulary used?
- Are sentences well-linked and varied?

Conventions (Punctuation)

- Are there sentence fragments or run-ons?
- Is punctuation correct and appropriate?

Writing Checklist

Use this form as needed to review student work and progress.

Name: _____ Date: _____

Title: _____ Genre:_____

Skill	Excellent	Fine	Needs Improvement
Stays on topic			
Clear purpose or point			
Supporting details; specific examples			
Logical development			
Main idea paragraph			
Transition words, phrases, sentences			
Clear expression of ideas			
Complete sentences			
Varied sentence types and structures			
Correct usage			
Conventions			

Comments: _____

_____

_____

_____

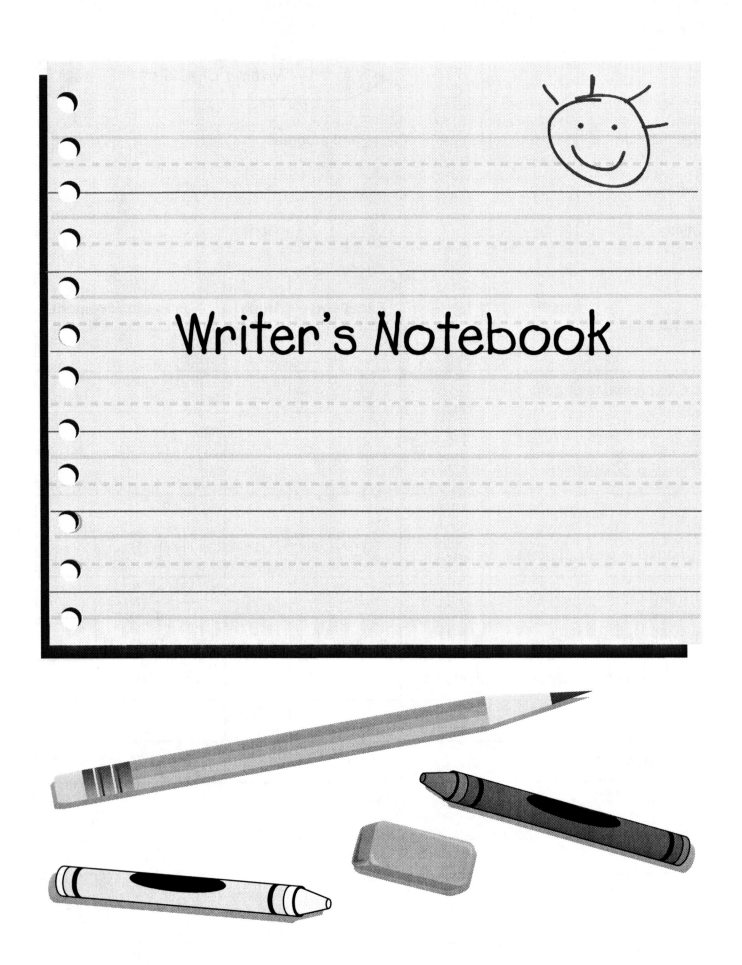

Writer's Notebook

How to Use the Writer's Notebook

A writer's notebook is a useful tool for all writers. Adapt the notebook pages to fit the needs of your class, adding or deleting pages to correspond to your curriculum.

Materials:

- pages 246, 248, and 249 (kindergarten)
- pages 246 and 248-251 (first grade)
- pages 246 and 249-255 (second grade)
- pages 246-247 and 249-255 (third grade)
- 1 folder or binder per student, to serve as a notebook

Directions:

1. Duplicate the relevant sheets, one set per student. (You might also wish to include some or all of the Classroom Display Cards on pages 208-240 or the various writing webs and word lists scattered throughout this book.)
2. Staple each set of sheets into a folder or punch holes to add the pages to a binder.
3. Distribute a notebook to each student.
4. Review the contents of the notebook. (See page directions below.) Do not review the contents all in one sitting, since that will overwhelm the students. Go over the pages one sheet at a time, perhaps when a related skill is being taught.
5. Refer to the sheets frequently, particularly when you are beginning your writing program. Help the students to become familiar with their notebooks so that they become a regular reference tool.

Directions Per Page:

The ABCs (*pages 246-247*): Allow students to keep these copies of the alphabet with them at all times for reference as they learn to form their letters. Even students who have mastered the alphabet sometimes draw a blank when forming a particular letter.

Words I Know (*page 248*): Emerging writers can keep a list of every new word they learn. You might even refer to this as "owning words," letting students know that once they own a word, it is theirs to use forever. Encourage students to see how word-rich they can become over the year.

My Dictionary (*page 249*): Duplicate several pages per child, letting him or her write new words in the blanks. The white spaces can be used either for illustrations of the words (for emerging writers) or definitions (for more fluent writers).

Parts of Speech (*pages 250-253*): Begin the lists of words as a class. Let the students add words while working in small groups. Instruct them to add more words as they learn or remember them. To help them build their lists, circle interesting words when responding to their writing. Suggest they copy those words on the relevant notebook pages.

Bubble Outline Form (*page 254*): Show the students how to write a topic in the first bubble and three supports in the remaining bubbles. Details per support should be written on the extending lines. This form can be used when writing a three-paragraph essay. It is wonderful for helping students to visualize the organization of ideas in a piece of writing.

Extended Bubble Outline Form (*page 255*): Use this like the previous form, but for an extended, five-paragraph writing. This form allows the writer to include an introductory paragraph, three supporting paragraphs, and a concluding paragraph.

The ABCs (Printing)

The ABCs (Cursive)

Words I Know

_____   _____

_____   _____

_____   _____

_____   _____

_____   _____

_____   _____

_____   _____

_____   _____

_____   _____

_____   _____

_____   _____

_____   _____

My Dictionary

Parts of Speech

Nouns

words that name a person, place, thing, or idea

Pronouns

words used in place of a noun

Parts of Speech

Verbs

words that show action or a state of being

Adjectives

words that describe a noun or pronoun

Parts of Speech

Adverbs

words that modify (describe) a verb, adjective, or other adverb

Prepositions

words that show how the object and another word are related

Parts of Speech

Conjunctions

words that connect other words

Interjections

words used to show strong emotions

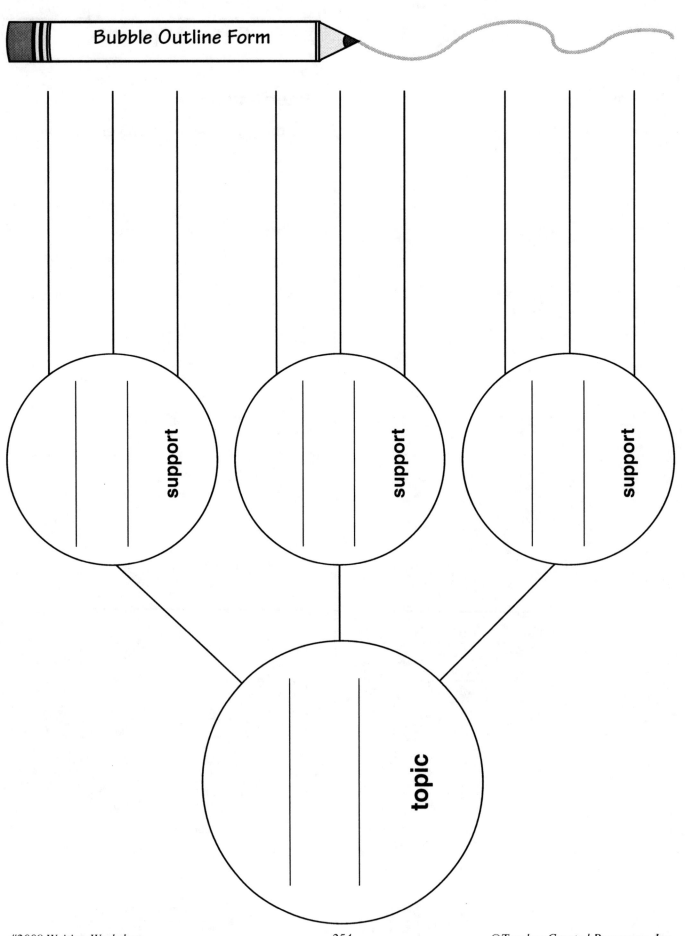

Bubble Outline Form

support

support

support

topic

Extended Bubble Outline Form

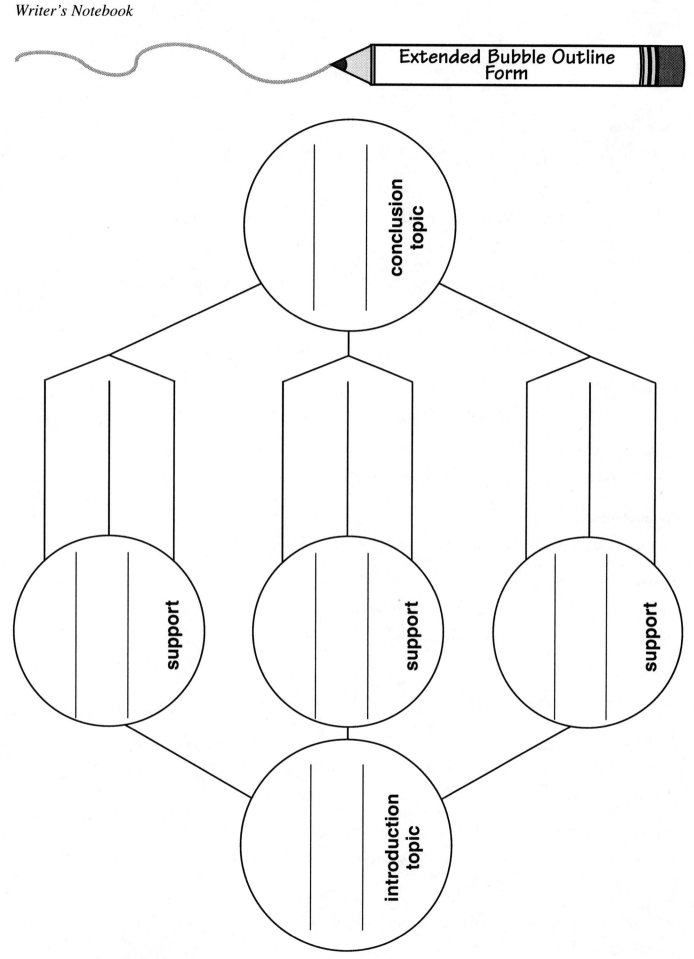

conclusion topic

support

support

support

introduction topic

Adjectives

Heller, Ruth. *Many Luscious Lollipops: A Book About Adjectives.* Putnam Pub. Group, 1992.

Adverbs

Heller, Ruth. *Up, Up, and Away: A Book About Adverbs.* Putnam Pub Group, 1991.

Antonyms

Berenstain, Stan and Janice. *Inside, Outside, Upside Down.* Random House Books, 1968.

Beginning Writing Workshop

Duke, Kate. *Aunt Isabel Tells a Good One.* Dutton Children's Books, 1992.

Elements of a Story

Duke, Kate. *Aunt Isabel Tells a Good One.* Puffin, 1994.

Expository Writing

Unwin, Charlotte. *Let's Pretend.* Dial Books For Young Readers, 1989.

Homophones

Bourke, Linda. *Eye Spy: A Mysterious Alphabet.* Chronicle Books, 1991.

Nouns

Heller, Ruth. *A Cache of Jewels and Other Collective Nouns.* Putnam Pub Group, 1989.

Heller, Ruth. *Merry-Go-Round.* Grosset and Dunlap, 1990.

Pronouns

Allard, Harry. *Miss Nelson Is Missing!* Houghton Mifflin Company, 1985.

Verbs

Terban, Marvin. *I Think, I Thought and Other Tricky Verbs.* Houghton Mifflin Company, 1984.

Writing Genres

Ahlberg, Janet. and Allen *The Jolly Postman.* Little, Brown, 1986.

Unwin, Charlotte. *Let's Pretend.* Dial Books For Young Readers, 1989.

Letter Writing

Ahlberg, Janet and Allen. *The Jolly Postman.* Little, Brown, 1986.